# 15 Days of Prayer
# With Saint Katharine Drexel

Also in the *15 Days of Prayer* collection:

*Saint Teresa of Ávila*

*The Curé of Ars*

*Pierre Teilhard de Chardin*

*Saint Bernard*

*Saint Augustine*

*Meister Eckhart*

*Thomas Merton*

*Saint Louis de Montfort*

*Saint Benedict*

*Charles de Foucauld*

*Saint Francis de Sales*

*Johannes Tauler*

*Saint Dominic*

*Don Bosco*

*Saint Alphonsus Liguori*

*Saint John of the Cross*

*Saint Thérèse of Lisieux*

*Saint Catherine of Siena*

*Saint Bernadette of Lourdes*

*Saint Thomas Aquinas*

*Saint Elizabeth Ann Seton*

*Saint Faustina Kowalska*

# 15 DAYS OF PRAYER
## WITH
# Saint Katharine Drexel

LEO LUKE MARCELLO

Liguori
LIGUORI, MISSOURI

Published by Liguori Publications
Liguori, Missouri
http://www.liguori.org
http://www.catholicbooksonline.com

*Imprimi Potest:*
Richard Thibodeau, C.Ss.R.
Provincial, Denver Province
The Redemptorists

**Library of Congress Cataloging-in-Publication Data**

Marcello, Leo Luke, 1945–
      15 days of prayer with Saint Katharine Drexel / Leo Luke
Marcello. — 1st ed.
          p. cm.
      Includes bibliographical references.
      ISBN 0-7648-0923-7 (pbk.)
      1. Drexel, Katharine Mary, Saint, 1858–1955—Meditations. 2.
Spiritual life—Catholic Church. I. Title: Fifteen days of prayer with
Saint Katharine Drexel. II. Title.

BX4700.D77 M37 2002
269'.6—dc21                                              2002073014

Printed in the United States of America
06 05 04 03 02    5 4 3 2 1
First edition

# Table of Contents

# How to Use This Book

AN OLD CHINESE PROVERB, or at least what I am able to recall of what is supposed to be an old Chinese proverb, goes something like this: "Even a journey of a thousand miles begins with a single step." When you think about it, the truth of the proverb is obvious. It is impossible to begin any project, let alone a journey, without taking the first step. I think it might also be true, although I cannot recall if another Chinese proverb says it, "that the first step is often the hardest." Or, as someone else once observed, "the distance between a thought and the corresponding action needed to implement the idea takes the most energy." I don't know who shared that perception with me but I am certain it was not an old Chinese master!

With this ancient proverbial wisdom, and the not-so-ancient wisdom of an unknown contemporary sage still fresh, we move from proverbs to presumptions. How do these relate to the task before us?

I am presuming that if you are reading this introduction it is because you are contemplating a journey. My presumption is that you are preparing for a spiritual journey and that you have taken at least some of the first steps necessary to prepare for this journey. I also presume, and please excuse me if I am making too many presumptions, that in your preparation for the spiritual journey you have determined that you need a guide. From deep within the recesses of your deepest self, there was something that called you to consider Katharine Drexel as a potential companion. If my presumptions are correct, may I congratulate you on this decision? I think you have made a wise choice, a choice that can be confirmed by yet another source of wisdom, the wisdom that comes from practical experience.

Even an informal poll of experienced travelers will reveal a common opinion; it is very difficult to travel alone. Some might observe that it is even foolish. Still others may be even stronger in their opinion and go so far as to insist that it is necessary to have a guide, especially when you are traveling into uncharted waters and into territory that you have not yet experienced. I am of the personal opinion that a traveling companion is welcome under all circumstances. The thought of traveling alone to some exciting destination without someone to share the journey with does not capture my imagination or channel my enthusiasm. However, with that being noted, what is simply a matter of preference on the normal journey becomes a matter of necessity when a person embarks on a spiritual journey.

The spiritual journey, which can be the most challenging of all journeys, is experienced best with a guide, a companion, or at the very least, a friend in whom you have placed your trust. This observation is not a preference or an opinion but rather an established spiritual necessity. All of the great saints with whom I am familiar had a spiritual director or a confessor who journeyed with them. Admittedly, at times the saint might well have traveled far beyond the experience of their guide and companion but more often than not they would return to their director and reflect on their experience. Understood in this sense, the director and companion provided a valuable contribution and necessary resource.

When I was learning how to pray (a necessity for anyone who desires to be a full-time and public "religious person"), the community of men that I belong to gave me a great gift. Between my second and third year in college, I was given a one-year sabbatical, with all expenses paid and all of my personal needs met. This period of time was called novitiate. I was officially designated as a novice, a beginner in the spiritual journey, and I was assigned a "master," a person who was willing to lead me. In addition to the master, I was provided with every imaginable book and any other resource that I could possibly need. Even with all that I was provided, I did not learn how to pray because of the books and the unlimited resources, rather it was the master, the companion who was the key to the experience.

One day, after about three months of reading, of quiet and solitude, and of practicing all of the methods and descriptions of prayer that were available to me, the master called. "Put away the books, forget the method, and just listen." We went into a room, became quiet, and tried to recall the presence of God, and then, the master simply prayed out loud and permitted me to listen to his prayer. As he prayed, he revealed his hopes, his dreams, his struggles, his successes, and most of all, his relationship with God. I discovered as I listened that his prayer was deeply intimate but most of all it was self-revealing. As I learned about him, I was led through his life experience to the place where God dwells. At that moment I was able to understand a little bit about what I was supposed to do if I really wanted to pray.

The dynamic of what happened when the master called, invited me to listen, and then revealed his innermost self to me as he communicated with God in prayer, was important. It wasn't so much that the master was trying to reveal to me what needed to be said; he was not inviting me to pray with the same words that he used, but rather that he was trying to bring me to that place within myself where prayer becomes possible. That place, a place of intimacy and of self-awareness, was a necessary stop on the journey and it was a place that I needed to be led to. I could not have easily discovered it on my own.

The purpose of the volume that you hold in your hand is to lead you, over a period of fifteen days or, maybe more realistically, fifteen prayer periods, to a place where prayer is possible. If you already have a regular experience and practice of prayer, perhaps this volume can help lead you to a deeper place, a more intimate relationship with the Lord.

It is important to note that the purpose of this book is not to lead you to a better relationship with Katharine Drexel, your spiritual companion. Although your companion will invite you to share some of their deepest and most intimate thoughts, your companion is doing so only to bring you to that place where God dwells. After all, the true measurement of a companion for the journey is that they bring you to the place where you need to be, and then they step back, out of the picture. A guide who brings you to the desired destination and then sticks around is a very unwelcome guest!

Many times I have found myself attracted to a particular idea or method for accomplishing a task, only to discover that what seemed to be inviting and helpful possessed too many details. All of my energy went to the mastery of the details and I soon lost my enthusiasm. In each instance, the book that seemed so promising ended up on my bookshelf, gathering dust. I can assure you, it is not our intention that this book end up in your bookcase, filled with promise, but unable to deliver.

There are three simple rules that need to be followed in order to use this book with a measure of satisfaction.

*Place:* It is important that you choose a place for reading that provides the necessary atmosphere for reflection and that does not allow for too many distractions. Whatever place you choose needs to be comfortable, have the necessary lighting, and, finally, have a sense of "welcoming" about it. You need to be able to look forward to the experience of the journey. Don't travel steerage if you know you will be more comfortable in first class and if the choice is realistic for you. On the other hand, if first class is a distraction and you feel more comfortable and more yourself in steerage, then it is in steerage that you belong.

My favorite place is an overstuffed and comfortable chair in my bedroom. There is a light over my shoulder, and the chair reclines if I feel a need to recline. Once in a while, I get lucky and the sun comes through my window and bathes the entire room in light. I have other options and other places that are available to me but this is the place that I prefer.

*Time:* Choose a time during the day when you are most alert and when you are most receptive to reflection, meditation, and prayer. The time that you choose is an essential component. If you are a morning person, for example, you should choose a time that is in the morning. If you are more alert in the afternoon, choose an afternoon time slot; and if evening is your preference, then by all means choose the evening. Try to avoid "peak" periods in your daily routine when you know that you might be disturbed. The time that you choose needs to be your time and needs to work for you.

It is also important that you choose how much time you will spend with your companion each day. For some it will be possible to set aside enough time in order to read and reflect on all the material that is offered for a given day. For others, it might not be possible to devote one time to the suggested material for the day, so the prayer period may need to be extended for two, three, or even more sessions. It is not important how long it takes you; it is only important that it works for you and that you remain committed to that which is possible.

For myself I have found that fifteen minutes in the early morning, while I am still in my robe and pajamas and before my morning coffee, and even before I prepare myself for the day, is the best time. No one expects to see me or to interact with me because I have not yet "announced" the fact that I am awake or even on the move. However, once someone hears me in the bathroom, then my window of opportunity is gone. It is therefore important to me that I use the time that I have identified when it is available to me.

*Freedom:* It may seem strange to suggest that freedom is the third necessary ingredient, but I have discovered that it is most important. By freedom I understand a certain "stance toward life," a "permission to be myself and to be gentle and understanding of who I am." I am constantly amazed at how the human person so easily sets himself or herself up for disappointment and perceived failure. We so easily make judgments about ourselves and our actions and our choices, and very often those judgments are negative, and not at all helpful.

For instance, what does it really matter if I have chosen a place and a time, and I have missed both the place and the time for three days in a row? What does it matter if I have chosen, in that twilight time before I am completely awake and still a little sleepy, to roll over and to sleep for fifteen minutes more? Does it mean that I am not serious about the journey, that I really don't want to pray, that I am just fooling myself when I say that my prayer time is important to me? Perhaps, but I prefer to believe that it simply means that I am tired and I just wanted a little more sleep. It doesn't mean anything more than that. However, if I make it mean more than that, then I can become discouraged, frustrated, and put myself into a state where I might more easily give up. "What's the use? I might as well forget all about it."

The same sense of freedom applies to the reading and the praying of this text. If I do not find the introduction to each day helpful, I don't need to read it. If I find the questions for reflection at the end of the appointed day repetitive, then I should choose to close the book and go my own way. Even if I discover that the reflection offered for the day is not the one that I prefer and that the one for the next day seems more inviting, then by all means, go on to the one for the next day.

That's it! If you apply these simple rules to your journey you should receive the maximum benefit and you will soon find yourself at your destination. But be prepared to be surprised. If you have never been on a spiritual journey you should know that the "travel brochures" and the other descriptions that you might have heard are nothing compared to the real thing. There is so much more than you can imagine.

REV. THOMAS M. SANTA, CSsR
LIGUORI, MISSOURI
FEAST OF THE PRESENTATION, 1999

# A Brief Chronology of Saint Katharine Drexel's Life

**1858:** Katharine Drexel is born to Francis Anthony Drexel and Hannah Jane Langstroth Drexel in Philadelphia on November 26. Hannah dies five weeks after childbirth, and the baby, along with three-year-old sister Elizabeth, is cared for by her father's brother and sister-in-law until Francis remarries.

**1860:** Francis A. Drexel marries Emma Bouvier.

**1863:** Younger sister Louise Drexel is born. The three little girls grow up in one of the most remarkable families possible: vast wealth and profound holiness. Emma becomes known as "Lady Bountiful" in Philadelphia, where at the porch of the family home she gives of her abundance to the poor. For some time, Francis is banking partner of J. Pierpont Morgan. He is said at times to have been instrumental in helping the United States Government through financial difficulties. He also leaves an indelible mark upon his daughters, praying before going to work in the mornings, making music on the organ in the private chapel in the family home, entertaining illustrious guests nightly at the formal dining table. The three young Drexel women experience the holiness of communal feasts and the elegance of all that dignified wealth could bring. Their parents inculcate in their daughters a sense of the great value of their faith. Francis reminds them to marry wisely and not to marry "worldly princes."

**1870's:** In 1870–71, two important facts: Young Kate learns of Hannah's existence and death in childbirth, a shocking discovery for the twelve-year-old. Also, Francis buys and rebuilds a ninety-acre country estate in Torresdale, Pennsylvania, as a summer home for his family. The family refers to the home as the "nest." Father James O'Connor, frequent visitors to the Drexel home and parish priest, becomes Kate's spiritual director. Emma encourages Kate and Elizabeth to help her with her philanthropic efforts at their home. Continuing their own education with private tutors, they also begin a Sunday school for other children. In 1874–75, the family takes trips to England and Europe. Kate continues to prepare for her formal debut into Philadelphia society, an event that she scarcely mentions in her personal journal.

**1879:** Emma becomes ill. An operation uncovers terminal cancer.

**1880:** Emma writes a letter to her daughters, "My Own Darlings, Last night I had a dream...." The family takes trips in attempts to get Emma the best medical treatment. Kate takes care of her dying mother, praying about life's meaning and purpose and considering a call to a life of prayer.

**1883:** Emma dies. The family takes trips to Europe and various parts of the United States, including Yellowstone National Park.

**1885:** Francis dies, leaving behind a famous will that makes news across the country. Two priests, Joseph Stephan and Martin Marty, visit the young Drexel women with a proposal to help people denied rights because of who they are. The three sisters respond, visiting reservations known to the two priests, and decide to build schools and provide for the needs of these people who were being treated unjustly. In 1886, Kate also buys a three-story house in Philadelphia as a school for African-American children.

**1886–87:** Kate's health takes her abroad for a "European cure," but she also has in mind to research educational systems. In a private audience with Pope Leo XIII (probably January 27, 1887), she asks for missionaries. He stuns her with the invitation, "My child, why don't you become a missionary?" It is an important moment in her life, going against her previous notions of who she was. In her private journal, she records her first reaction as leaving the papal audience in tears. She prays. Then something happens. Her life is never the same after this encounter.

**1887:** The Drexel sisters make a trip to the Dakotas, where she meets Chief Red Cloud. It is he who will later declare that he would fight his own people if he had to in order to protect the "blackrobes," her missionary sisters. Soon she is buying land and building schools.

**1888–89:** Kate experiences many twists and turns in spiritual direction under Father James O'Connor, first in the decision to become a religious, then in the decision to found a missionary order for "Indians and Colored," in the language of the day.

**1889:** Louise marries Edward Morrell. Six months later, Kate enters Mercy Novitiate in Pittsburgh and is received into the novitiate as Sister Mary Katharine (the name that she always preferred to her baptismal name, Catherine Mary).

**1890:** In January Elizabeth marries Walter George Smith, attorney to the widow of Ulysses S. Grant and to Jefferson Davis. In May Katharine's former spiritual director (now Bishop of Omaha) James O'Connor dies. Then in September, Elizabeth and premature baby, Joseph, die. Louise and Sister Mary Katharine inherit even more of the family fortune and continue Elizabeth's work with such charitable projects as St. Francis's Industrial School at Eddington, Pennsylvania.

**1891:** Mother Katharine professes vows as the first member of her new order known as "Sisters of the Blessed Sacrament for Indians and Colored People." In July the cornerstone for the new motherhouse is laid, and the sisters are threatened with violence. Sisters begin to travel to various parts of the country to establish schools, such as in Santa Fe, New Mexico. In 1895 Louise establishes St. Emma's at Belmead, Virginia, a school for young black men. SBS schools are soon founded in numerous places.

**1904:** Mother Katharine travels through the South. Her brother-in-law Edward Morrell addresses the House of Representatives for full voting rights for African Americans. Mother Katharine establishes schools in places that strike out against her efforts for people being denied education because of their color. Her efforts in Nashville prove powerful against the racial hatred of the day.

**1912:** Mother Katharine becomes gravely ill and nearly dies in Albuquerque, New Mexico, no doubt having contracted typhoid and pneumonia in her strenuous work elsewhere.

**1901:** Friend and coworker Monsignor Joseph Stephan, Director of the Bureau of Catholic Indian Missions, dies.

**1913:** Rome gives final approbation of the rule for her order.

**1915:** In New Orleans, Xavier High School, the normal school, is founded. Brother-in-law Edward Morrell dies.

**1918–1920's:** Mother Katharine travels through the Louisiana bayous founding rural schools, and she travels extensively in other places as well, founding schools and helping others in need. In 1925 she sends sisters to help a school already established in Sacred Heart Parish in Lake Charles, Louisiana. Here, as elsewhere, a number of future church leaders have their first contact as children with the SBS, including future bishops Leonard Olivier and Harold Perry, future Sisters of the Blessed Sacrament, and distinguished lay leaders.

**1932:** On the occasion of the formal dedication of Xavier University, she is interviewed by Gwen Bristow in New Orleans.

**1935:** In St. Louis, Missouri, she suffers the first of two serious heart attacks that will change her life. After the second heart attack, she is forced to curtail her activity and is confined to the motherhouse in Bensalem for the rest of her life.

**1943:** Mother Katharine undergoes surgery for cancer. Later that year her sister Louise dies suddenly of a stroke. It is yet one more serious loss in Mother Katharine's long life.

**1955:** On March 3, Mother Katharine dies. Immediately people are talking about the death of their saint. Crowds line up to pass by her body in the chapel of the motherhouse, and then crowds fill the cathedral in Philadelphia for the funeral.

**1964:** John Cardinal Krol declares open the cause for her canonization.

**1973:** Her writings are approved by the Congregation of the Causes of the Saints.

**1987:** Pope John Paul II declares her Venerable.

**1988:** The pope declares her Blessed.

**2000:** On October 1, she is canonized in Rome, along with one hundred Chinese martyrs, Saint Bakhita, and Saint Maria Josefa del Corazón de Jesus.

# Introduction

KATHARINE DREXEL, perhaps like all saints, offers us a unique approach into the universal call to holiness. Every life is unique, filled with its own dilemmas and graces, yet every life comes from the same infinite source and hears in its deepest heart the call back to that source. How each of us responds to that call is part of our unique identity, but not every one of us answers the call with such an openness of heart. The writings and life of Saint Katharine Drexel reveal a thoroughly human person, a thoroughly holy person. She offers us a view of someone so much like us yet unique at the same time. Her life and words reveal a heroic life, yet perhaps nowhere in her writings is she more profound than when she reveals her grappling with the daily struggles of the spiritual life. She was a person of her times yet a person ahead of her times. She is a thoroughly American saint, as well as a thoroughly universal saint. She was one of the wealthiest people in U.S. history. She offers us one of the supreme examples of poverty lived for the sake of the Gospel. Over the vast span of her long life of nearly ninety-seven years, she experienced great losses and faced profound sorrows. At the same time, she said with all honesty and candidness, "I am, and have always been one of the happiest women in the world." What does she have to say to us today? Hers is one of the great stories of the past that transcends itself. Hers is one of those great stories that can inspire future generations. Hers is one of those great lives that can help center us in the present struggles of our own lives. "Peacefully do at each moment what at that moment needs to be done." This quotation will be found as the meditation for Day 15 in this book, and that is the direction and thrust of these fifteen days: to bring us back into the daily life in which we are immersed and help us live the Gospel message as we find ourselves confronting it. We are all called to holiness, but our roads look so different. Perhaps there are many individual paths, but for Katharine Drexel, there is only one way to God, and that is with an open heart.

The overall movement of this book will be from our individual call to holiness through the ordinary experiences of human relationships, the social world of which we are a part, and the spiritual dimensions of every aspect of our lives as we discover them leading us to a greater love of God. Over the course of fifteen days, we will meditate on our individual call to holiness, our first recognitions of such calls, and the obstacles that keep us from entering fully into the mystery of grace into which we are invited. Katharine Drexel was drawn to live the contemplative life yet fully lived a missionary life. Long before Thomas Merton wrote his book *Contemplation in a World of Action*, she was living it. Her life, like ours, contained paradoxes. How she met them is in part a measure of her individuality. It is also evidence of her universality.

The famous American writer Henry David Thoreau wrote that he went to the woods to live simply. In *Walden* he claimed that a person's wealth can be measured by the things that a person can live without. There is perhaps no better example of American individuality than Thoreau. Katharine Drexel occupies an interesting place in American history. She is kin to Thoreau with his bold and searching spirit. Like Thoreau, and certainly outdistancing him in her vision of justice, she is a pinnacle of the American spirit.

Philanthropy, however, was not among Thoreau's favorite experiences. Clearly, Katharine Drexel exhibits a unique example of a person at home with wealth and with poverty. She was born into the same spirit of simplicity as the early settlers of this country. Her natural mother, Hannah Jane Langstroth, may very well have contributed to Kate's inclination toward simplicity, but her father's wealth gave her a taste for all of the finest things in life.

Yet poverty has a significantly different appeal for her than it had for the famous visitor to Walden Pond. Her delight in temporal goods was a hallmark of the good life that she knew from childhood. To appreciate what one has demands an ongoing disposition of gratitude, and it was that gratitude that kept her close to the Eucharist. The things of the world are valuable in so far as they "bring us and many others...to the same eternal joys for which we were all created."

If her call to holiness was manifested amid a lavish childhood, so was her attraction for human relationships. She learned early the needs of people living in her city. With her sisters, she helped her mother give to the poor. Her sense of justice developed out of her appreciation first of all for the gifts of her life and the loving environment of her family home. Her training was to be mindful of what was at hand, and she learned to write letters at a very early age. Soon she became aware of the differences among people. At the age of twelve, she had an important early encounter with the uncontrollable twists of life, a discovery that would have profound influences upon her later choices.

As an adult, she would much later learn that the world was often not like the loving environment of the Drexel home. So when she encountered racial hatred aimed at destroying her work, she met it not with shock and ignorance but with the loving attitude that her parents had instilled within her from her earliest years.

The movement traced here is the spiritual awakening of a sense of justice in a world torn by differences and fraught with obstacles for a person desiring to find one's way to God. The recurring question is, "What is that way?" Katharine's life is always Christ-centered, and the Eucharist is never far from that center. Yet there are human dilemmas that weave their way through our lives. Friendships develop. Friends die. Loss is inevitable. Sadness and joy seem like companions in life, linked inevitably in the way of the cross.

But the cross is not the end. Humility is not some puritanical punishment to keep a person from enjoying life. True humility is the attitude of a heart that wishes to be carried back to God, lightened of its unnecessary baggage but honest in its acknowledgment of its limitations, its resistance to accept inevitable suffering, it joyfulness in embracing everything.

To die to everything in life is not to give up on everything. Rather, the great wealth of Katharine Drexel was transformed into a great wealth for others. Her sharing of the bread of her life was an extension of her desire to share of her wealth with those who did not have. It was also her way of sharing her appreciation for the existence of others who exhibited thankfulness in their lives for whatever gifts *they* had received.

For Katharine Drexel, there were many ways to live out thankfulness. "The quietest way is the best," she wrote. Clearly, she was not one to blow the horn in the temple when she offered her gifts. There are times to make a glad sound, and there are times for silence. All of the movements of her life followed the deep desire in her heart for a greater love for her beloved, for a more intimate prayer life.

Her life and writings reveal this movement: the more she prayed to love, the more she loved to pray. Her prayer might happen as she was scrubbing the floor on her hands and knees. It might happen as she celebrated a great banquet for a friend on his jubilee anniversary. It happened, of course, in her time of thanksgiving after receiving the Eucharist. But her heart was a heart on the move. "Arise from your Christmas thanksgiving," she urges her followers. "Arise from the Holy Communion to find Him in the people...."

Along the way, we will encounter obstacles. No matter, she reminds us: Proceed peacefully in everything we do. If we arise from our eucharistic thanksgiving and go into the world seeing "every single event in life" as coming within the will and providence of God, how can we be anything else but peacemakers?

The challenge to peacefulness is formidable. So is the way to

God. It is awesome. It is also our path. "All do not go by the same path," Katharine wrote, but we have been created to follow our Lord on this path. Why would anything else matter? We are called to holiness. We are called to love. We are called to bring God's peacefulness into the world. As it came on that first Christmas, so will it come again and again in our hearts. If our hearts are open and we pray, we will find ourselves in God's infinite mercy and love. "Blessed are the peacemakers," Jesus tells us, "for they will be called children of God" (Matthew 5:9). In Katharine Drexel's eyes, we are all children of God.

# Abbreviations Used in This Book

B      Bristow, Gwen. *Interview with Mother Katharine Drexel.* New Orleans *Times-Picayune*, 15 November 1932, 1+.

D      Duffy, Sister Consuela Marie, SBS. *Katharine Drexel: A Biography.* Bensalem, PA: Mother Katharine Drexel Guild, 1987; originally published in 1966.

P      *Praying With Mother Katharine Drexel: Taken From Her Writings*, research by Sister M. Thomasita Daley, SBS, preface by Sister M. Georgiana Rockwell, SBS. Bensalem, PA: Mother Katharine Drexel Guild, 1986.

R      *Reflections on Life in the Vine, Found in the Writings of Mother M. Katharine Drexel, Foundress of the Sisters of the Blessed Sacrament.* Bensalem, PA: Mother Katharine Drexel Guild, 1983.

UAR  Unpublished letters and papers in the Archives of the Sisters of the Blessed Sacrament, Bensalem, PA.

V      *Prayers Heard, Miracles Performed: A Special Presentation With Angela Hill.* Video. New Orleans: WWL TV, 2000.

There are three major texts that I have used for my meditations upon the writings of Saint Katharine Drexel. Two of these are compilations of passages from her writings, selected and published by the Sisters of the Blessed Sacrament. The third major text is the official biography written by Sister Consuela Marie Duffy, SBS, published in 1966.

There are many other sources that have led to my meditations in this book, however. I have been praying with Katharine Drexel since the 1980's when I became interested in her life and work. The original research for my first book on Katharine Drexel, *Blackrobe's Love Letters*, focused on primary and secondary materials in the Archives of the Motherhouse of the Sisters of the Blessed Sacrament in Bensalem, Pennsylvania. The initial research for that book was made possible by a Sherman Research Fellowship. I wish to thank the Sisters of the Blessed Sacrament and the Drexel Archives for permission to study, use, and quote from their sources. I especially thank Sister Margaret O'Rourke, SBS, Sister Therese Misencik, SBS, Father Don Piraro, Father John Giles, and Stephanie Morris for their encouragement and assistance.

# 15 Days of Prayer
# With Saint Katharine Drexel

## DAY ONE

# Call to Holiness

## FOCUS POINT

Our lives offer many choices, and we are not inclined to every invitation with the same willingness and determination. In fact, some invitations do not seem like attractive opportunities at all. We would rather not go to a certain place or a certain meeting or associate with particular people or circumstances. Something rubs us the wrong way or repels us like the wrong end of a magnet, and we say to ourselves, "This is not what I had in mind. I am going north, not south, east, not west." Suddenly, we find that what we had planned is not the best way to get to the place we had been longing for. More surprisingly, we may sometimes begin to wonder if the path that we have been traveling will lead us to that place at all. We might be faced with an important decision, and what seemed like a good choice for someone else might not seem like a good choice for us at all. We are all called to holiness, but our steps along the path—perhaps even our paths themselves—are different.

*It is a lesson we all need—to let alone the things that do not concern us. He has other ways for others to follow Him; all do not go by the same path. It is for each of us to learn the path by which He requires us to follow Him, and to follow Him in that path. Let us remember our Master's injunction, and we shall be saved from many pitfalls: "What is it to you? You follow me" (John 21:22). [9R]*

*I love to think how small the little foot of Our Lord was on that first Christmas. A little foot does not make big strides; it can only take little steps. In imitating the Divine Babe, let us place ours in His footsteps. Then we shall, with God's grace, grow into the bigger footsteps and make greater strides. If we are faithful in little, we will obtain grace for the big. [3R]*

*All holiness consists of participating in the holiness of Jesus Christ, the Son of God. [8P]*

A re all of us called to sainthood? Is every call different? Clearly, when we look at the people around us, it is easy enough to see that there are vast differences within human nature. Some people seem holy in one way, whereas others may exhibit holiness in a vastly different way. We may say that we believe in the communion of saints, but we somehow see them as far away from our ordinary lives. Saints may have seemed heroic to us in ways that are impossible for us.

When we hear people say, "My mother was a saint" or "Aunt Mary was a saint," do we believe such claims, or might we suspect that such people are confessing their own limitations in comparison to someone who has inspired them? We might even doubt the claim to holiness, believing instead that such claims are really veiled indictments of someone else. "Aunt Mary was a saint" might translate "Uncle John was a tyrant."

On the other hand, there are those among us who genuinely inspire us with their lives. Perhaps we really do believe that our aunts or our grandfathers or our uncles or sisters are saints. We know in our hearts that they had an intimate relationship with God that radiated throughout their lives and touched us and other people. These are the people who continue to inspire us long after they are dead. We believe that they are among the communion of saints, yet we still feel their lives were different from ours. They were called to holiness in the circumstances of their lives and have transcended this world. They may no longer be in this world in the way that we have to be. Yet the memory of such lives brings back to us the reality of their struggles. They lived and struggled, and in the ways that each of them responded they found the graces to live the lives which were theirs.

Over the course of our lives, we are faced with many questions and decisions. What should we do? How will our decisions affect the rest of our lives? Some decisions seem to have great weight. If we do this, perhaps that will happen. If we don't do this, perhaps something else will happen. Often it seems impossible to predict the consequences of our choices. So what shall we do, and how will we reach the outcomes that we believe are desirable?

At certain times it is apparent that we are being spiritually challenged. We had planned to go in one direction, yet important forces seem to be inviting us, maybe even impelling us, in another direction. Saying yes may not be easy, and our dilemma may not even be a choice between one thing and another, between one path and another. Sometimes the sheer complexity of our lives seems beyond choice. We know that life offers more possibilities, and we don't know how to embrace them. At such times, however, we may have an instinctive urge, a barely conscious understanding that we are being called to a greater life than we are living. For those of us who believe in God, we come to the conclusion that this desire must come from God and that if we are open to the invitation we will be given the grace to discover what we are now to do.

Katharine Drexel faced many questions in her lifetime and many challenges in those questions. How would she meet these challenges, and how would she know if her answers to these questions would lead her closer to God? Perhaps her willfulness and her pride would give her momentary gain but eternal loss. She learned much from her father, Francis Anthony Drexel, a wise and holy man, an eminently successful businessman and banking partner of J. Pierpont Morgan. She understood gains and losses. She could have taken over her father's business. In fact, she did manage his fortune. After his death, she and her sisters inherited incredible wealth, and they were faced with the challenge of how to use and manage their inheritance.

Yet a bigger question had already challenged her. Two years before her father's death, Katharine had faced the death of Emma Bouvier Drexel, the woman who had raised her and whom she had believed to be her mother. During the three years of Emma's terminal illness, young Katharine cared for her beloved Emma and prayed. What was God telling her in this difficult period? For all of the Drexel wealth, money could do nothing to assuage Emma's pain or prevent Emma's death. During this time, Katharine often thought of the contemplative life. Perhaps God wanted her to spend the rest of her life in prayer. A cloistered life of prayer seemed possible, certainly desirable. Perhaps in this desire was a call from God.

Yet Katharine had always assumed that she would follow Emma's footsteps into Philadelphia society. Known as "Lady Bountiful," Emma had a long history of helping the poor of their city. The three young Drexel daughters helped give out material goods to the poor who regularly lined up at their door, and Katharine and her sisters had already begun as children to teach others about the mysteries of her faith. Life, however, had seemed certain in some of its expectations. The young woman had been given much. They would enter society and continue to return their gifts to those less fortunate.

Fortunately for Katharine, she had also begun spiritual direction at a very young age. Her childhood notebooks are filled with the declarations of her resolution to become a better person, indeed a holy person. Katharine loved life. She knew that there were obstacles greater than some of her strong temptations, stronger than the chocolate that she enjoyed, stronger than parties and horseback riding, fine clothes, good food, extensive travels, illustrious friends. Anyone reading little Katie's childhood journals might at first find amusement. The child's resolution to give up sweets for the remainder of the year might not sound like much evidence that a future saint is forming, yet in every small decision that she made was the strengthening of her faith that would grow into the heroic steps she made later in life.

Years later, after she had decided to use her wealth to help people denied education and rights because of their particular ethnic backgrounds, she went to Rome where in a private audience with Pope Leo XIII she asked him to send missionaries to the United States. When he turned the tables on her, telling her that he had none to send and inviting her to become a missionary, she fled in tears, as she reports in her journal. That was not what she thought God had been telling her all of her life. Perhaps a cloistered life, perhaps the married life, perhaps grandchildren, but missionary? The idea did not seem to fit the path—or any of the paths—that she had been traveling in her life so far.

That papal audience was a turning point in her life. She prayed about the experience. She prayed to understand her tears and the invitation that seemed to come out of the blue. It was in the course of this difficult period of prayer that she found her answer. What did all of those things that she had formerly considered mean in light of the ultimate goal that she had always known was hers. She had known from her earliest years that God was calling her to holiness, yet she had not understood that the call might just as easily come from one direction as another. "What is it to you?" she heard the Lord say. "You follow me."

So she followed the direction of her heart in these prayers. The next steps required enormous courage. She had no idea where the steps would lead, yet she took the first, submitting herself to the Sisters of Mercy, soon afterwards initiating the Sisters of the Blessed Sacrament, a step that had seemed not only impossible but against all of her prior instincts. She had not seen herself in such a light, but the light came. She accepted the challenges, and the rest of the story is history, a remarkable history.

We are all called to holiness, but not all paths are alike. My choices and my possibilities might be very different from my neighbor's. For those of us who follow Jesus, the image of the Divine Babe may seem very far removed from these choices and possibilities. It is important for us to remember that those examples of sanctity or heroism that inspire us were not people born fully grown as adults. They started out with basic needs: the need to learn to walk and to talk, to find the right path for them upon which to walk and to learn how to use their minds and their senses as they walk along the path. As they grow, children explore the world, and often they get hurt in the process, playing with fire, or making foolish mistakes, such as trying to eat insects. Athena might have been born full bloom out of the mind of Zeus, but wisdom comes slowly to humans. So too must sanctity. The lives of the saints remind us of the many steps that holy people take before they reach holiness. Indeed, the writings of many saints suggest that so long as they live holy people continue to take steps toward the holiness to which they are called. Katharine Drexel wrote, "All holiness consists of participating in the holiness of Jesus Christ." Jesus was born a baby. If we wish to follow in the steps of Jesus, we must first learn to walk.

## REFLECTION QUESTIONS

What are the things that I do not have the courage to let alone, the things that do not concern me? We are all called to holiness, and some paths are fine for other people, but what is my path? Have I honestly discerned the path for me? Are there still pitfalls in my path? Do I let other people's concerns obstruct me from following Jesus? I know that some of my journey has been in little steps, but do I expect only big steps now? Are the small steps I'm taking leading to holiness or merely to self-centeredness? How do my choices reveal that I desire to participate in the holiness of Jesus Christ? Do I really believe that my neighbor is also called to holiness? Do I respect the paths of others even when those paths may seem alien to mine?

## DAY TWO

# Poverty

## FOCUS POINT

Things are essential in our lives. Most of us would say that we need a bed to sleep in, food to eat, a refrigerator in which to keep the food, a telephone, clothes, a watch, eyeglasses. Sometimes the tension to pay the bills to supply these needs becomes a great burden. As a result, we desire more money to take care of these and other needs. We want to be comfortable. We know that desiring "things" or riches can get us into spiritual trouble, yet we do not yearn for poverty. We certainly do not pray to become poor. Still we need many things in life. Nevertheless, poverty is itself a gift.

*Give me, through Mary, the gift perpetually to live and realize with ardent faith (even if I am bereft of feeling it) that You are my supreme good, source and center of all good, the only good, the only perfect good. This will give me the gift of detachment from all things on earth—the FRANCISCAN POVERTY—to be attached to You perpetually. [12P]*

*How truly was the Cave of Bethlehem the great educator of the world. [20R]*

*Temporal things, after all, are only to be valued inasmuch as they bring us and many others—as many as possible—to the same eternal joys for which we were all created. [21R]*

———

Why do we want things? As children we made our Christmas wish list. As adults we continue to dream about possessing things we do not yet have. "Keeping up with the Joneses" may be a cliche; yet, even after we have supposedly made progress in the spiritual life, we find ourselves looking enviously at others who have things we do not possess. Sometimes the things we envy are not tangible things. In the great sonnet that begins "When, in disgrace with fortune and men's eyes, / I all alone beweep my outcast fate," Shakespeare laments the emptiness of begrudging others the things they have, even the way that they envision life or seem to be richer in hope. At such times of envy, nothing consoles. There is no "thing" that will fill the void of despair. Shakespeare concludes the poem with the supposedly chance thought of the beloved, and in the thought the poet no longer envies the wealth of others. The thought, even the mere memory of love, restores the abject person, now freed from sorrow and no longer possessed with the sense of having nothing.

What does it mean to be wealthy? In the world's sense of the word, that means to possess things. Yet wealth is of course relative. A person who is in debt for five million dollars considers finding ten thousand dollars in a forgotten bank account as little, whereas the person who makes twenty thousand dollars a year would feel differently about suddenly discovering an account containing such a sum. Perhaps it is understandable that the poor might sometimes pray to become rich, despite Jesus' warning about the rich person's difficulties in entering heaven. For those who are not well off, it might seem very odd indeed that a wealthy person might pray to be unattached to wealth, to be in fact poor.

Katharine Drexel did not pray to be rich. She was born wealthy. Her childhood home had many wonderful things in it. Daily her parents prayed in their private chapel, appointed with marble and gold. Nightly her parents entertained illustrious dinner guests. Her father's business partner was often at the table, eating fine food and drinking great wine. Little Katie's clothes were elegant. Family photographs show the three little girls dressed in expensive fabrics, looking like members of a royal household. In Venice the family stayed at the Hotel Danieli. At home the little girls had private tutors and governesses and a stable of horses.

Ironically, among the things that Katharine Drexel left behind are pencil stubs, shoes mended with string, a primitive wheelchair made from an ordinary chair. Yet Mother Katharine was not one of those rich eccentrics whose lives are reported in the media. When she went through leftover food in the kitchen of her order's motherhouse, she was genuinely looking for scraps of food to save that she might eat, not making some public statement. When she used a scrap of paper to write out one of her meditations, she was simply aware, like Beethoven who sometimes wrote a theme or motif on a napkin in a bar, that one took what was at hand and made the best use of it. Waste did not make sense. She was thoroughly practical, though nonbelievers and believers alike might say hers was a practicality beyond ordinary practice.

Few of us will ever be as wealthy as Katharine Drexel. Even if we find ourselves wealthy, we do not desire to let go of everything. We have responsibilities for our children or for our aging parents or with our jobs. As we grow older, we want to simplify our lives, but our needs seem to become even more complicated. For most of us, we think that if the mortgage were paid, the children educated, the credit cards wiped clean, we would be free of the fear of not having enough money. Yet some of us who have these "things," enough retirement money coming in, children who have good jobs, and the means of taking care of the grandchildren, still want more.

Even if we could be detached from the things of this world, we would not pray for poverty. To be poor is to be disenfranchised, is it not? Who would plan on giving birth today without a plan for where the delivery would take place? Mary and Joseph lived in different times, of course, to be sure; yet their situation is a challenge for us to imitate. We don't want our children or our grandchildren to be born in a cave. Such a scenario is unlikely, but the model remains. We don't want the risks of poverty. We want to count on a good education for our children. We don't want to sleep on a mattress that might aggravate our back trouble. We have to get our eyes checked to make sure we are not developing cataracts or glaucoma. Our children need good nutrition, not cheap fast-food calories. We have to dress properly on the job, perhaps paying expensive dry-cleaning bills if we want to keep our jobs and get raises to match the rising cost-of-living expenses of maintaining a car or meeting the house payments.

When Mother Katharine was visiting one of her schools, she refused the sisters' offer of their bed for the night. She insisted that they were the ones who needed the good night's sleep so that they could be good teachers the next day. She slept on the floor because her sisters had a need greater than hers. She was not being heroic or making a public statement of her holiness. She did without when doing without made sense. She understood comfort. She had grown up with it. She knew what she was doing without.

Yet she also knew what was the greatest use for what she had been given. She gave freely and generously when the gift made sense. If someone wrote to her asking for money, she considered the need. If the need were reasonable or just, she answered with the gift; whenever she gave, she also reminded the receiver that there were no guarantees that there would be more money. If she were to die, for example, there would be no more money. She would do what she could do while she could do it.

When her good friend Monsignor Joseph Stephan approached the fiftieth anniversary of his ordination, Mother Katharine spared no expense in the surprise celebration for him, her longtime friend who was now suffering. For her own anniversary, she wanted no celebrations. The Cave of Bethlehem was good enough for her Lord. The floor and leftovers were good enough for her when such conditions were necessary. Yet she ordinarily slept in a bed, ate normal meals, and took care of the business still in her care, at least for as long as she could. She dispensed her personal wealth to those in need, and she did so with the idea that these gifts would help such people help themselves to a greater dignity as human beings. That work is another integral part of her story and her spirituality.

But as a human being, she lived her long life with an awareness of the need for things and always with a prayerful attitude of the need for detachment from things in so far as they kept her from centering her life on the greatest good. She shared her wealth so that others might have joy, not mere joy in the things of this world, but in the joy of being a human being, in the joy of loving.

## REFLECTION QUESTIONS

What is my relationship to the things in my life? How do I use these things? What is their relationship to the center of my life? Have I ever prayed for "things" that I do not have? Have I ever prayed for poverty? Am I conscious of detaching myself from the things that keep me from the true center of my life? What lesson can I learn today from the Cave of Bethlehem? Do I appreciate the gifts of my life? Do I bring joy into the world? Among the people that I know, does my life contribute joy? Do I share my temporal things? With whom and why? Are there others who could benefit from my sharing of these things? Does my sharing with others contribute to the "same eternal joys for which we were all created"?

# DAY THREE

# Justice

## FOCUS POINT

We want justice. We say that our demands for justice are demands for what is right. Sometimes, however, confusion results. What we feel we deserve or what we feel our enemies deserve may be at odds with what we believe is right. Sometimes we think that people get what they deserve. Often we have to admit that people do not get what they deserve. There are some people who do not believe that they deserve hell. There are others who cannot believe that they deserve goodness and as a result condemn themselves to misery, sometimes even condemning themselves more harshly than they judge their enemies. A generous heart cannot accept either of these extremes. It is not a question of being lukewarm. Jesus condemned the lukewarm, neither the hot nor the cold. Generosity of heart begets more love, and love begets justice. If we live the Gospel, we will be people of justice, and our lives will bring good news to the poor.

*My Beloved Spouse, did I not give you everything You asked me here? You love those missions so much do You think that when You are continually with me I will give you less? For You can lean Your head on my breast, and You can love me—love me with all You want. Do You think I would refuse then anything You asked me for those two Races? [21P]*

*Infinite Justice, I deserve hell but I shall look and dwell on Your infinite mercy and love. [22P]*

W e have all heard the expression "just desserts." Are we happy when our enemies get what we think they deserve? Do we really want for ourselves what we ourselves deserve? How many times have we read in a saint's life "I deserve hell"? It is not an uncommon sentiment to find in saints' writings, yet sometimes we doubt the authenticity of such a statement. We might ask ourselves whether this is some kind of false modesty. Did these so-called holy people really believe that they deserved hell? Not to understand oneself can lead to serious spiritual problems. Not to acknowledge one's goodness might even be a sin of pride. Indeed, what does such a claim say about a particular saint's view of the rest of us sinners? If the saint believes that he or she deserves hell, then are all the rest of us condemned too since we know that we do not meet the standards of those great lives?

We have learned that someone as apparently so peaceful as Mother Teresa of Calcutta had her moments of darkness, moments in which she felt abandoned. Did she doubt God's love? Saint Teresa of Ávila also experienced such dark times, and she too often felt that there was not a balance in the relationship with her beloved. Of course, the saints recall for us in their writings their awareness that there cannot be equality in this kind of relationship. When a person is aware of one's own imperfections and is in a loving relationship with One who is perfect, how can there be a balance? Something will always be unequal. Something will always be out of joint. My gifts to my beloved can never match my beloved's gifts to me. My love can never match my beloved's.

All in all, infinite love is hard to fathom. So too is infinite justice. Katharine Drexel gives us a superlative example of a life grounded in a firm sense of justice and a life radiant with its living out that justice in its day-to-day work.

Katharine Drexel was willing to give everything away. Like Saint Francis, she had known expensive clothes. When faced with poverty in Philadelphia, Emma Bouvier Drexel had given out clothes and food from the porch of the family mansion. Beside her on the porch were the three little Drexel girls. They learned early to give of what they had, and they learned early that there were great inequalities in life, great injustices. "Lady Bountiful" Emma Drexel was called by the Philadelphians that she served with love.

After her father died, Katharine accepted the invitation of Father Joseph Stephan and Bishop Martin Marty to visit the people of the Dakotas, people who had been denied many of their basic needs, though they had been promised much by the government that had taken their lands and forced them to live in harsh conditions. She and her sisters responded to the needs of these people and fought the injustice that was holding them captive to indignities. Soon after her father's death, she bought a big house in Philadelphia and turned it into a school for children denied education because of the color of their skin. The story of the contributions of the entire Drexel family—Francis, Emma, Elizabeth, Elizabeth's husband, Katharine, Louise, and Louise's husband—is truly a remarkable story of a family's generous gift of itself to those in need. Ten percent of Francis's will went immediately to charities. At the time of her death, Emma was caring for a large number of families in Philadelphia and had already dispensed a vast amount of her wealth to the poor. The lives of the three daughters and the two sons-in-law reveal great generosity toward peoples denied basic rights. Indeed, both sons-in-law fought for the rights of such people. The lives of the three Drexel sisters are exemplary in their generosity.

How could Katharine Drexel say to her beloved, "Infinite Justice, I deserve hell"? Her life has been thoroughly examined. Clearly hers was a holy and heroic life, yet her claim cannot be ignored. It stands parallel with such a statement in the writings of many saints and cannot be dismissed as inauthentic.

What is justice? The word *justice*—the Latin word *iustitia* translates as justice, fairness, or equity—contains the word *just*, in Latin *ius*, which translates as right or law. When Katharine Drexel addresses the beloved as Infinite Justice, she is not speaking of a made law, yet she does not seem to be speaking of equity either. With God there can be no equal. What is right or fair in the eyes of God?

Jesus said, "Blessed are those who hunger and thirst for righteousness, for they will be filled" (Matthew 5:6). Katharine hungered for justice, and she fought the long struggle against injustice. In the intimate relationship with her beloved, she understood the essential inequality between them. She was willing to give her beloved everything, and she could rest her head upon her beloved's shoulder, just as she could say in prayer, "You can lean Your head on my breast, and You can love me—love me with all You want." Love is reciprocal. Nothing is to be refused. Love bestows its own gifts.

The nature of her beloved's love is infinite, yet she knew that human love is limited. So too she knew that human justice is limited. She knew that the world did not always honor its claims to justice. Again and again, she went to the aid of people denied what was justly theirs. She did so not because she expected anything in return. She did so because she lived and worked for what she believed was right and fair.

Katharine Drexel's life gives us something even more striking than her profound generosity. A century before the United States came to reflect and implement justice in its laws for minorities, Katharine Drexel actively fought racism in her own quiet and radical way of living out the Gospel. She was directly responsible for opening and/or supporting many schools and missions across the United States. At the time of her death, more than sixty such centers stood as evidence of her ongoing apostolic work, including Xavier University of Louisiana, the only predominately African-American Catholic institution of higher learning in the United States.

She fought for what she knew to be right. Her way is often characterized as a quiet way, but it is always a strong and powerful way. Radical? Yes, it was radical in its day and in its quiet power, but Katharine thoroughly lived it out of her profound experience of the Gospel.

For Katharine Drexel, there was no dichotomy between the infinite justice of God and the human justice that we are called to make happen in the world. There cannot be one set of standards for justice in the realm of the divine and another in the world of humanity. Such a division means injustice. In the Gospel of Luke, we learn about the rejection of Jesus at Nazareth when he read the passage from Isaiah in the synagogue: "The Spirit of the Lord is upon me, because he has anointed me to bring good news to the poor. He has sent me to proclaim release to the captives and recovery of sight to the blind, to let the oppressed go free, to proclaim the year of the Lord's favor" (4:18–19). Katharine Drexel saw injustice. Far ahead of her time, she worked in her quiet and effective way for what she knew in her heart to be right. She lived the Gospel, and her life brought good news to the poor.

## REFLECTION QUESTIONS

What is my sense of justice? Do I fight against injustice, or do I remain silent? Do I do nothing in the light of injustice in my neighbor's life yet expect justice for myself? Do I make decisions in my daily life that are consistent with the Gospel? How am I called to be a more just person? Does my life bring good news to the poor? How am I called to make the world a more just place?

## DAY FOUR

# Love of My Enemies

## FOCUS POINT
Early in life we learn the distinction between "them" and "us." Later in life, we learn that there are actually people in the world who are not only different from us in some way but people who hate us. One reason that some people give for not following Jesus is the command to love one's enemies. Such people claim that to turn one's cheek is to be foolish and weak. When we look at what Jesus' enemies did to him, we have to ask ourselves, "Why should I love my enemies?" My enemies would stop my work and mock what I hold sacred. They attempt to make me helpless in the world, yet I must love them and to love them might mean my destruction.

*They say, "There is another place on the city's outskirts" for our educational work. How truly was the Cave of Bethlehem the great educator of the world! This was indeed the School of the Immaculate Mother.... [20R]*

*O glorious Queen of Martyrs, help me to fight bravely against my enemies—the devil—the world and myself...that I may be generous and devoted in the service of your Divine Son. [15P]*

H istory tells us that enemies exist. As children, we learn early that someone might take our toys without regard to our relationship to these things. We learn that people can claim relationships in a similar way. Our classmate in the first grade betrays us in the second grade. A teacher in the third grade selects a student as his or her favorite. What once seemed like the natural order of things is turned upside down. Children's games reveal the incipient animosity of pitting one person against another, one group against another. "Red Rover, Red Rover, let Johnny come over." Sides reapportion themselves, fortified with new identities. Year after year, we learn the new ways an old dynamic works: them versus us.

When we are young, it is easy enough to see how someone different can be our enemy. People may make fun of me because I go to a church that to them seems strange. In earlier days of our history, children might have been embarrassed by their parents' or grandparents' accents. Perhaps the lunch the little girl took to school seventy-five years ago smelled odd to her classmates, flavored with seasonings from her immigrant mother's kitchen so very different from their own mothers' kitchens. The word "foreigner" made many children cringe in those days, and fear of being thought different reinforced many immigrant parents' desire for their children to be American, not aliens. In World War II there were many people who fought against this kind of stereotyping with as much vehemence as they fought an "enemy" across the water.

It doesn't take us long in life to realize that our enemies do not have to be different from us. One of the shocking lessons in life is to discover that someone who does not look or sound like an enemy can hate us. An enemy can be someone who we assumed loved us. Our neighbor might call the police to complain about us or even sue us. Our brother or sister might steal from us or betray us in an even worse way. We might discover that we are also capable of being an enemy, not only to others, but to ourselves. Not only might we have to face that "otherness" in ourselves—the ways that we are seen by others—but we might also have to admit that we have become our own worst enemy, an idea that might sound cliché but only because we have lived past the initial shock of such a discovery.

History indeed teaches us that enemies exist. How we deal with them may tell us more about ourselves than about them. It is understandable to feel a repulsion for one's enemies. It may even seem natural to strike out at that which threatens us. Is hatred natural? We find ourselves challenged all of our lives with a dilemma: How can I coexist with my enemies yet still accomplish my life's work? Even greater is the challenge to love my enemies. In this regard, to follow Jesus seems to make no sense.

Katharine Drexel had enemies. When she and the Sisters of the Blessed Sacrament were preparing to lay the cornerstone of their new motherhouse in 1891, there were threats that they would be destroyed. Her brother and her architect devised a plan to protect them. For the celebration of the laying of the cornerstone, they placed a small locked box in a prominent place with a warning sign: "Do not open. High explosives. Nitroglycerine." The dedication took place, and everyone was safe.

Inside the locked box were wooden broom handles.

In Texas once, the KKK threatened the sisters because of their plans to educate African Americans. The story goes that the sisters prayed for protection and the Klan headquarters, struck by lightning, burned to the ground.

Enemies, however, are not always duped by our stratagems nor struck by lightning. Sometimes they seem to thrive, even outliving us, burying us, enslaving our children, rewriting history, profiting and feasting on golden plates in their marble palaces.

Katharine Drexel knew her enemies. Once in a series of strategic moves in Nashville, Tennessee, she fought racial hatred in order to build schools for young African Americans, who the city fathers had decided did not need an education. She was a shrewd businessperson and in 1907 worked legally to secure the property and build the Immaculate Mother Academy. Yet after her success, she was saddened by the continuing hatred evident in her enemies, and she wrote to one of her chief opponents expressing her compassion for his pain. He retaliated by publishing her letter in the newspaper, saddening her all the more at the continuing hatred. There was nothing else she could do with his hatred, but she could celebrate the success of her work. The school opened, and the young people benefited from her courageous efforts. She was not helpless in the face of her enemies. She was hated, but her work flourished.

We do not always see our work flourishing in the sight of such hatred. People gassed in concentration camps remain signs of someone's malicious victories. Yet the malicious victories that we find in history also have their own lessons. Hitler's bunker went up in flames, even if there are people who would rewrite history to suit their own purposes.

Survivors of atrocities often find it difficult to hear the exhortation to love one's enemies. Some would argue that to love those who have destroyed my people is not to honor my people. To turn the other cheek is to ask to be destroyed myself. Yet Jesus was not asking us to make ourselves an unthinking victim of our enemies. Following the lead of Walter Wink, Robert Barron in *And Now I See…A Theology of Transformation* has pointed out that if someone has struck you on the right cheek, to turn your other cheek means to take a stance that prevents the enemy from striking you in the same way again, in fact, to present a stance that defies a subsequent blow.

Yet on the cross Jesus seems helpless. He is unable to take another stance of any kind. He has been rendered helpless in the world. Has he? The cross offers us some profound questions and answers. We will look at these questions in another chapter. Here we must admit several things: We have enemies. If we do not deal with them, we will be destroyed. On the other hand, we may find ourselves destroyed even if we deal with them. By many standards, to love my enemies really seems to make no sense.

An important question here is, "Who are my enemies?" Praying to the Mother of Martyrs, Katharine Drexel prayed "to fight bravely against my enemies—the devil—the world and myself...that I may be generous and devoted in the service of your Divine Son." The devil is not some Halloween myth with a pitchfork. With regard to her enemies, she seems to include both the world and herself in the company of the devil. It is easy enough for us to see evil at work in our world. The enemy threatens to bomb us. The enemy humiliates us in public. The enemy calls us names or dismisses us as fools or weaklings. It is also easy enough at times to see that I am my own enemy. Some people will even admit to being their own worst enemy. It doesn't take a wise person to reach such an admission. Sometimes the mere circumstances of our lives force us into admitting that we have put ourselves into a foolish position, sometimes even a dangerous position, sometimes even a self-destructive position. Once we grant that evil exists—and there are of course those who would not grant that— we can easily enough see how it manifests itself in the world and in our own lives. We don't have to point the finger only at "them." We must admit that there are also times when we have to point the finger at "us."

So where is the wisdom in this command to love one's enemies? If I am looking for results—and Saint Katharine Drexel was often looking for results of her efforts—I have to acknowledge that not all of my efforts will meet with success. Sometimes evil will have its day. Sometimes the people I love will sin against me. Sometimes I will betray others; sometimes I will betray even myself. Why should I love my enemies who hurt me? Why should I love myself when my actions are foolish or self-destructive? Because someone who died on a cross has told me that I should? Do

I want to die on a cross? No, of course not. Jesus didn't want to either. He prayed on the night before he died, "My Father, if it is possible, let this cup pass from me" (Matthew 26:39), and again on the cross, he cried out, "My God, my God, why have you forsaken me?" (Matthew 27:46). He had not asked to be destroyed. He had turned the other cheek, yes, but he also stopped one of his followers from further violence when Peter severed an ear from the enemy.

We are not called to be passive weaklings, but a fact of life is that we are sometimes vulnerable. All in all, it is more important to stand our ground in light of who we are, not to deny who we are or what we are about, and what we are about is love. It is more important to love than to strike the winning blow. This idea is one of the hardest among Jesus' commands.

In one passage from the Gospel, a rich young man walks away, unable to give up his riches. Katharine Drexel had no difficulty in giving up her riches, but her life presented challenge after challenge in loving her enemies. She succeeded in becoming a more loving person. Her generosity led to her greater capacity to love, and her growing love kept her ever more focused on the service of her Beloved. To love our enemies might look like weakness in the eyes of the world. In truth, however, it is our strength.

## REFLECTION QUESTIONS
Who are my enemies? Do I love my enemies? Do I understand the ways that I can be my own enemy? Do I love myself and my neighbors even in the face of my own and their destructive capabilities? Do I turn the other cheek as a sign of my solidarity with Jesus? Am I courageous in facing my enemies? Can I accept the possibility of defeat for the sake of love? Is it more important for me to win than to love? I know that God wants my best efforts to yield fruit, but when I see the fruit dying on the vine or destroyed by blight, do I lose heart or do I turn, like Jesus in the garden or on the cross, in prayer? Do I pray for my enemies?

## DAY FIVE

# Friendship

### FOCUS POINT

We are not alone in our journey but travel with companions. Sometimes we have the sense of solidarity with others; that is, we realize that we are traveling along the same path toward the same goal. Other times we are aware of the distance in time and place between us and our friends. They may be farther along the journey, perhaps even gone ahead of us in death. To be aware of friendship is also to be aware of loneliness, for to lose a friend is to lose our traveling companions. In one sense, we are indeed alone on our journey. In another, if we have ever had good friends, we will never be alone on our journey, even when our friends are gone or even dead.

*I will follow You in the company of others, ever before me the greater glory of God. [23P]*

*I saw them in their agony. I saw them in their agony, those great souls [Monsignor Stephan and Bishop Marty]! [Duffy 358]*

---

One of the seemingly strange injunctions in the Gospel is that we not invite our friends to dinner: "When you give a luncheon or dinner, do not invite your friends or your brothers or your relatives or your rich neighbors, in case they may invite you in return, and you would be repaid" (Luke 14:12–14). Rather, we are to invite those who have no way of paying us back for what we do. Yet Jesus also speaks about the persistent friend at the door, a friend that might even appear in the middle of the night with a request (Luke 11:5–8). What is the nature of a good friendship? The Latin writer Cicero knew its qualities and rewards, but then also gangs and tyrants know the value of human relationships.

There are many kinds and degrees of friendship. The longer we live, the more we learn about these differences. A childhood friend may change schools or move away, and later if we have the chance to get together, we may wonder why we were so close to someone so different. School reunions, whether for high school or college, might bring us to similar conclusions. Who has changed the most? Perhaps we reach a different conclusion. Perhaps the passage of time confirms how much we were alike and in some core way are still alike. In some friendships the passage of time highlights the differences, and we no longer feel the earlier bond. In some friendships the passage of time seems not to have affected the bond at all. With such friends we might sit down and talk as if months or years have not passed, as if we are catching up on the latest news even though the news is now old.

Some friendships endure time and differences. Others do not. The end of a friendship can come suddenly, as in death or a violent disagreement. Some friendships become stronger when tested by difficult times. Like gold in the fire, some friendships prove their mettle, enduring and becoming even more beautiful. We value these relationships as we grow older, especially as they begin to disappear with the deaths of our friends. We also lament the deaths of friendships that do not endure the fire, those that melt away in the difficult times, revealing themselves for what they are, not gold, not everlasting.

That is not to say that such friendships might not have had a worthwhile place in our lives. There are some relationships that are important to us at certain stages of our journey. Perhaps a mentor or a teacher or a spiritual director becomes a friend in the process of our limited relationship. The college teacher who announced to his class that he was not going to be anyone's friend in the class was no doubt establishing boundaries, yet he was also denying the inevitability of what happens in human relationships. Simply put, there are some people that we are naturally inclined to like and others that we must exert effort in order to maintain an amicable relationship. We don't have to be friends with people that we see daily, such as those with whom we work, though it helps if we can be cordial. We might even find a personal relationship with a mentor or teacher or spiritual director a liability or a hindrance to the professional relationship. Yet with the passage of time, relationships do change, and the most professional therapist might become a client's friend, showing up at a wedding years after the therapy has ended. There are too many factors to predict when friendships will or will not develop, will or will not endure. Some friendships even develop into something else. There are some people who describe their spouse as a best friend, whereas others might laugh at such an idea. There are just as many definitions of love as there are of friendship.

For all of the differences of kind and degree in friendship, there are some constants. There must be some degree of affection, and there must be some degree of responsibility. In some friendships the word "love" makes sense. In others, it does not. "We are just friends," I might say when someone asks whether I am romantically interested in someone else. "We are just keeping company" might sound like an old-fashioned way to describe a relationship that is not explicitly romantic.

The word "company" has developed new connotations in our time. To be a company man or a company woman does not suggest friendship. On the other hand, to be a companion suggests warmth and understanding. To accompany someone means to walk with that person, to travel along the same journey.

Katharine Drexel appreciated the nature of human relationships. They are gifts from God that help us see the way. When we travel with others along the journey, we feel reassured. There is someone to watch the suitcases while we go to the restroom in a foreign airport. There is someone to call when we hear bad news and need to talk it over with an understanding friend.

Perhaps Jesus is not eschewing friendship in the injunction not to invite our friends to dinner. Perhaps the admonition contains the wisdom of not expecting a return for what we do. To invite someone to dinner because we want to be invited back is an ego-centered gesture. In my heart, I am offering to break bread with someone because I am hoping to get an invitation in return, not because I am giving freely. Katharine Drexel gave of her wealth with no expectation of return. She gave because she wanted to increase the numbers of people at the banquet table. She wanted others to taste of the goodness that she had experienced. She knew also that ultimately the shared banquet could only give greater glory to the One who had prepared the banquet to begin with. She was not the ultimate source, and she did not expect any glory in return. The more she gave, the more in awe she became of the endless gifts that were waiting for the hungry, uninvited of the world.

She was not one of the uninvited, however. Her life had been one of privilege and gifts. Beyond these circumstances, she could see that everyone ultimately was invited. Everyone might be a companion on the journey, rich and poor, the powerful and the powerless. At her Lord's table, everyone was invited; however, not everyone would answer the invitation. Not everyone would want to go on the journey. Not everyone wants to accompany us.

Thus it was that she could rejoice when she found herself in the presence of friends, not because she would receive anything from them in the realm of gifts or invitations, but because their presence was reassuring that she was not alone on the journey, alone with her gifts, alone in her joys.

One of the painful aspects of friendship is shared suffering. A mother suffers when her child suffers. Grown children eventually suffer when they see their parents old and suffering. Friendship, however, does not always contain that physical bond of blood kinship that leads us to care about one of our own because the sufferer is one of our own. Friendship comes with our choices, mutual choices. We choose to eat with these people. We choose to telephone them when we are in trouble or to spend vacation time with them or to reveal ourselves to them when we are helpless or confused or to give them gifts when we want to increase the happiness of their birthdays or wedding anniversaries.

Edward Albee's play *A Delicate Balance* begins with a couple's appearance at their friends' home. They have come because they can no longer bear to be alone at their own home. Life seems dark and meaningless. They arrive, asking to be taken in. Gradually, their friends come to understand that these two people mean to stay. The request is unconditional. We are here. We are asking to stay as long as we might need to, and we do not know how long that might be. It might be forever.

Jesus didn't tell us to give with a calculator in hand. He didn't tell us to give with an expectation of being repaid. In fact, the Gospel tells us to give with no expectation of return. Someone asks for my shirt, so I am to give my overcoat as well.

Friendship offers great consolations, but it also offers pain. Katharine enjoyed many great friendships in her long life. At times these friendships inspired her. At times they caused her anguish. Her great friend Monsignor Joseph Stephan suffered great physical and emotional pains near the end of his life. For his fiftieth anniversary as a priest, he found himself the recipient of a great banquet in the motherhouse of the Sisters of the Blessed Sacrament. Later from Germany where he was trying to recover his health, he wrote to his dear friend Mother Katharine about what was becoming an irreversible deterioration of his well-being, and Mother Katharine was helpless to do anything that might ease her friend's pain.

All in all, Katharine Drexel could celebrate those people who walked with her on her journey because she could see that their footsteps marked the way for her and for others. She thanked God for the gift of such friendships. She also thanked God for being able to see past the agony of these footsteps. We are not alone on our journey. We may be alone in our individual pain, beyond the help of others, but we are not alone in our agony. We are not alone in our joy.

## REFLECTION QUESTIONS

What are my expectations of friendship? Do I see the glory of God in my relationships with friends? When I see a friend suffering, what is my response to that person? When I have been helpless to do anything for a friend, what have I heard God saying to me? If a friend shows up at the door, making what seems like an unreasonable request, what is my first response? What would be the response of Jesus if such a person appeared at the door? Have I ever been such a person? What kind of friend am I? Do I help my friends along the way by my example? How am I called to be a better friend?

## DAY SIX

# LOSS

---

## FOCUS POINT

Who among us would want to be known as a person of sorrows? Yet during Holy Week, we hear about the Man of Sorrows, and in many cultures there are feasts honoring the Mother of Sorrows. Since sorrow seems to be an inevitable part of life, perhaps these images are models for us in our sorrow. Loss too seems inevitable, and no one wants to be a loser. Sorrow is a natural successor to loss. Is there any way around this chain of events? Loss seems to weaken us and make us less capable of devoting ourselves to what we think we ought to be doing. Yes, loss is inevitable, and no one wants to be a loser. Nevertheless, we can learn much about ourselves in such experiences of loss.

---

*And here is the passive way—be filled unto the fullness of God.* [13P]

*The passive way—I abandon myself to it, not in a multiplicity of trials, extraordinary penances accomplished, practices of great works—but in peaceful abandonment to the tenderness of Jesus, which I must try to imitate, and by being in constant union with His meek and humble heart. [24R]*

*What likeness is there between me and my Mother? Do I try to be like her, in her love for Jesus? In her devotion to the cause for which He died—the salvation of souls—in her absolute submission to the will of God, in her patient suffering? Holy Mary, Mother of God and my Mother too, let me stand at the foot of the cross with you, to learn its lesson and to learn to be like the Mother of Sorrows. Amen. [15P]*

From childhood we have heard the axiom: "It doesn't matter whether you win or lose. It's how you play the game." The advice smarts and stings our ego. Of course it matters that we win. Of course it matters that we lose. Yes, of course it matters how we play the game, but who wants to be a loser? Nobody. Surely the mechanism of loss and recovery is a natural part of life. We lose all manner of people, places, and things. An old man might lose his wife. A momentarily distracted mother loses her child in the department store. A teenager loses his best friend. A young child loses teeth. An old person loses teeth, hair, eyesight, hearing, taste, home, money. Some losses are more frightening, more debilitating, more irreversible than others. Other are merely annoyances, experiences to be lived through briefly until their resolution.

Saint Anthony has become the patron saint of lost things. Sometimes enlightened homilies have tried to reverse his status. We hear that Saint Anthony should not be relegated to the pantheon of plaster patron saints, treated like some clay god, the object of our superstition. Indeed, he is far too important, we are told, to be stereotyped as a useful trick to find car keys or lost wallets, yet we do have the need to call upon someone, something outside of us when we face a loss. To whom shall we turn when we are helpless in the face of loss? Saint Anthony has become a useful stopping place for some. The Psychic Hotline is a temptation for others. Still others crawl around on their hands and knees, determined to find the car keys themselves, determined to prove that there is only one way to recover our losses: "I can do this by myself." I! Me! On my own! After all, I am alone in my loss. No one else will understand. No one else cares. I am the one stranded with the car that will not start. I am the one whose credit cards may have fallen into a thief's hands. I am the one who will miss the lost and irreplaceable photograph.

A woman who had been devoted to Saint Anne all of her life heard a homily one day—on the feast of Saints Anne and Joachim, naturally enough—that tried to dispel the myths surrounding the parents of Mary. "No one even knows if Saint Anne really existed," said the young priest, determined to rid his congregation of superstitious devotions. What he neglected to acknowledge— long before he fell in love and left the priesthood and then the Catholic Church—was that Mary did indeed have a mother, and the image of a good mother for another good mother was just what the woman sitting the small chapel had needed to hear that day, not that such a woman had been invented by superficial believers. The distraught woman did not lose her need for such a role model. She went away that feast day, sad that the young priest had been so insensitive in his manner of teaching. Years later, she was able to understand that perhaps the name "Anne" was not the name of Jesus' grandmother. The woman continued to think of that woman as Saint Anne long after the young priest was no longer "Father." In fact, years later, she felt more than a twinge of sadness to have lost the young priest, sadder than she herself had felt faced with the possibility of losing her patron saint, acknowledging that the name itself didn't matter. She came to understand what she had needed, and she was honest about the need, and she knew what she couldn't afford to lose. The image of Saint Anne had carried the woman through difficult childbirths, through the childhood experiences of her own children on into her experiences later as a grandmother. To her, the young priest had become lost. He had become one of the lost children of the Church, for in truth, he had been a priest that she had genuinely appreciated, except for his dismissal of her patron saint. To her, his leaving was a loss to the Church, yet to him, this leaving might very well have seemed a gain.

We have learned in physics that for every action there is a reaction. We have been told that when one thing is destroyed there is a reaction. What is lost here in one part of the cosmos is found there in another part. The dynamics of love may throw this neat universe into confusion.

Life does not always seem to make sense.

Clearly, to have found our car keys may lead us to believe that Saint Anthony has led us to them. Some of us will say that of course he did. Others will say no. The young woman who prays to Saint Anne for a healthy baby rejoices when she counts her newborn's fingers and toes. She thanks God for intercession through Saint Anne on the happy occasion. We are relieved to find our watch, our ring, our credit-card-filled wallet, our child at the lost-and-found counter.

The dynamics of loss in our spiritual life do not necessarily imply an equation: loss equaling gain. If someone loses her purse in the parking lot, someone else might find it and restore it to its rightful owner; on the other hand, the finder might just as easily keep it. Some things lost can never be restored. Jesus reminds us that once salt has lost it taste, it will never be salty again: "Salt is good; but if salt has lost its taste, how can its saltiness be restored? It is fit neither for the soil nor for the manure pile; they throw it away" (Luke 14:34–35). This reminder in the Gospel of Luke precedes three other passages about loss: the lost sheep, the lost drachma, and the lost son. Unlike salt, however, which having lost its saltiness might as well be thrown away, the found sheep, the found drachma, and the found son are all occasions for rejoicing.

The parable of the Prodigal Son contains a number of points for meditation in regard to the idea of loss and recovery. At the resolution of the story, the father tells the older son that there is reason for celebration and rejoicing "because this brother of yours was dead and has come to life; he was lost and has been found" (Luke 15:32). In one sense the older brother's resentment throughout the story can be seen as resulting from his insecurity that he might lose his own place in the father's heart. In anger the older brother accuses the father of never having supplied such a feast for him. He does not mention the robe or the ring which the father bestows on the returning son, but clearly the older brother's resentment runs deep. The father, however, feels the loss of his young son in a profound way, and the degree of his rejoicing does indeed match the degree of mourning over that which had been lost, perhaps even exceeding in joy what he had experienced in loss during his son's absence. The story does not tell us about the father's feelings during the son's absence. Instead, it focuses on the son's dissolute living in a faraway place where he eventually loses all sense of self-respect and dignity. Once the son returns, however, the relationship among the three offers challenges for all three. The young son repents. The father accepts, blesses, and celebrates. The older son is invited to open his own heart. The story is filled with action, even at its conclusion which seems to leave us hanging. Does the older son open his heart? Do we?

Katharine Drexel sometimes spoke of "the passive" way. She was not referring to a state of doing nothing. In her reflections upon Mary's experience of losing her son, she saw this internal activity as consistent with the Annunciation. Mary's *fiat*—"let it be with me according to your word" (Luke 1:38)—is in one sense a passive acceptance of the will of God. In one of Mother Katharine's Communion reflections, we find the words "I no, not I, but WE" (13P). The passive means to "be filled unto the fullness of God." Yet Mary's abandonment of her own will—Let it be—is akin to Jesus' prayer in the Our Father: Your will be done. The movement within our hearts to open ourselves in loving relationship—"WE"—is our response to the invitation to open ourselves to another. As a response, it is an activity of my heart. As a loving abandonment of "me" for "us," it is a passive way for me to be, yet in Katharine's prayer, it is I versus WE, not me versus us. The "I" does not become an inactive object, but an active participant in the relationship, even though the "I" is no longer in control.

The older brother in the parable would like to be in control. He tries to persuade his father not to celebrate. Mary's first response is to question how such a thing as pregnancy can be since she has not known a man. Even in the garden, Jesus at first prays, "if it is possible, let this cup pass from me; yet not what I want but what you want" (Matthew 26:39). Matthew recounts how Jesus then re-entered the company of his disciples, though he finds most of them sleeping. He has a brief conversation with Peter about staying awake and then leaves Peter with the words, "the spirit indeed is willing, but the flesh is weak" (26:41).

Katharine understood the weakness of the flesh and the inevitability of human limitations. Loss is sometimes one of the most challenging experiences we face. We want back what we have lost. Sometimes what we have lost is someone else's gain. Sometimes what we have lost is no one's gain at all. In the parable of the Prodigal Son, all three participants have something to gain, whether it means being loved and accepted or growing as a loving and accepting person. In this story, what was lost is now found, and there is genuine cause for rejoicing.

What happens, however, when what is lost cannot be recovered? We may never find the lost one-of-a-kind photograph of our grandmother. We may never recover our vision or our health or our marriage or our prodigal children. "Daughters of Jerusalem," Jesus said, "do not weep for me, but weep for yourselves and for your children" (Luke 23:28). Jesus said these words on the way to Golgotha. He had been marked a loser, stripped of everything, even abandoned by his friends.

What does the Man of Sorrows say to us? "Do not weep for me, but weep for yourselves and for your children." Jesus redirects our attention away from mourning over what cannot be changed. At this point the cross is inevitable. However, the children, our relationship to the future, what is going to be, is not lost yet. Filled with pain, yes, tainted by the consequences of all that the past will bring upon it, yes, but the next generation, our children, the future—there is the cause for true weeping. The Man of Sorrows knows better than anyone else.

At the age of twelve, Katie Drexel discovered the facts about one of the major losses of her life. She learned about the loss of Hannah, the mother whom she would never know, the mother who had died five weeks after giving birth to her. Perhaps then it is not surprising that the Mother of Sorrows spoke so powerfully to Katharine. What is to be learned from the sorrows of motherhood? Katharine looked at the experience from both directions, as a child who had lost her mother and then for most of her life as Mother Katharine, the witness through many long years of the losses of those she loved: family, friends, sisters of her order, the beloved people who were the recipients of her many gifts. The image of the Mother of Sorrows spoke powerfully to her about the inevitability of such a witness. It also spoke to her of the holy call beyond that sorrow. Mary's example provided Katharine with a role model in her devotion to the will of God, in her selfless love in sharing Jesus with others for the sake of others, in her patience.

Clearly, a mother knows the pain of her children. She weeps for them, though she cannot prevent their suffering. She knows the inevitability of their losses. They will lose their teeth, lose sleep to their first nightmares, lose friendships, lose their childhood innocence, perhaps even lose hope in their own futures, and the mother cannot prevent these losses. She can stand by, be there, wait for their return, and like the father in the parable of the

Prodigal Son, she can rejoice when she sees the child returning. How much our God must rejoice when we return after our journeys or years of waste. It is never too late to return. Sometimes what has been lost cannot be found, but when it can be recovered, what joy, what blessings—to be a patient mother, to be the welcoming father—such waiting and acceptance may be what it means to stand by the cross. The loss is not the end of things. The waiting is truly a part of life. What we do with our losses says more about us than any loss we might experience. Saint Anthony holds a baby boy in his arms. Saint Anne stands beside a young daughter. These images are only plaster, yet there is something in the plaster that gives shape to our hope. Yes, plaster shatters. Hope can shatter too, but not when we place our losses in perspective. What do we really believe—that a plaster saint has performed a trick? Or that God has indeed been faithful to the promises of old? If we believe that we and the saints are in communion, that we are all recipients of God's ancient and ever-present promises, then we will not see ourselves as losers, even when what has been lost cannot be found. Furthermore, when we are losers, when what we have lost cannot be recovered, we can be strengthened, not weakened, by our loss if we follow the example of those before us like Mary in their love for others, their willingness to do God's will, and in their patience. "Let it be with me according to your word" (Luke 1:38).

## REFLECTION QUESTIONS

What have been the losses of my life? How do I deal with loss? Have I ever experienced the emptiness of loss only then to discover what it means to "be filled unto the goodness of God"? Like Mary, when have I ever said "Let it be according to your word"? When I have found such a prayer difficult? Am I at peace with the losses of my life? Who are the role models that have shown me a way to deal with loss?

## DAY SEVEN

# Sadness Versus Joy

### FOCUS POINT
A joyful heart is a loving heart, but a joyful heart has experienced its share of sorrow. There is a difference between genuine sorrow and a habit of mind that is sad, and what we do with our sorrow changes us.

*Please don't say that I had some great sorrow that drove me into a convent! I am, and always have been one of the happiest women in the world. I never had a sorrow in my life except those that must come to men and women who live long enough to outlive many of their loved ones. [B]*

*Heart of Mary, my Mother, transfixed with a sword of sorrow, enkindle with my heart, by your intercession, the divine fire which consumes your heart…. [15P]*

*Beware of sadness for it is contrary to love in diminishing and destroying its power of affection. [23R]*

---

There are reasons to be sad. Some reasons seem even beyond the pale of grief. The woman who learns that her unborn child has died within her has no consolation. There is further suffering ahead, for she must be delivered of her stillborn baby, and beyond that experience, there will be further sadness. How many women have demonstrated the power of their incipient motherhood by facing another pregnancy, and how startling is the hope of these women and men who dare to hope for new life once again, rather than to grieve for the rest of their days over what they have lost. There is no recovery of the dead, no undoing what has happened, no replacing one life with another. Every life is unique. Every loss is unique. No one can replace another. There are reasons to grieve at legitimate losses, and there are reasons to be honest about our feelings concerning such losses. If we do not come to terms with our losses, they will come back to visit us later in life. There are reasons to be sad, though a life overwhelmed with sadness will have little room for love.

The Gospel tells us that "Jesus wept" (John 11:28–37). At the death of his friend Lazarus, he was "greatly disturbed in spirit" at the sight of Mary's tears, and "deeply moved" he asked where Lazarus had been laid. Then, invited to go and see, Jesus "began to weep. So the Jews said, 'See how he loved him!'" The Gospel reiterates, "Then Jesus, again greatly disturbed, came to the tomb." Telling those with him to take away the stone, Jesus lifted his eyes, thanked the Father, and "cried with a loud voice, 'Lazarus, come out!'" (John 11:38–43). More than once, we hear that Jesus is "greatly disturbed" and expresses grief at the death of his friend and at the sight of those left behind to mourn. The account early on reveals that Mary's response was to go to Jesus, though observers thought that she was going to her brother's tomb. Clearly, there are reasons to be sorrowful, and this Gospel account has comforted many people in their grief, not only because of the raising of the dead Lazarus but because of the comforting presence of Jesus who weeps with us in our grief.

The movement of the account is toward thanksgiving, confidence, and belief. Jesus concludes the words of the prayer to the Father, "I have said this for the sake of the crowd standing here, so that they may believe that you sent me" (John 11:42).

Jesus acts out of his love for Lazarus as well as for the mourners left behind. There are reasons to be sorrowful, and weeping and sighing can be genuine expressions of our love. The account, however, takes Jesus and the mourners in this scene beyond their sorrow. The direction of the account takes the sorrow to Jesus, who shares it and who then takes it directly to the source of the sorrow, the dead man's tomb, and there, lifting his eyes, transforms it into a prayer of thanksgiving, trust, and love. With this prayer, Jesus then "cried with a loud voice" calling the dead back into life. Jesus is not calling in a loud voice merely because Lazarus is far away in the world of the dead. Jesus wants the others to hear, but he is truly crying out with a loud voice from the depths of sincere grief. The sorrow of Jesus has been transformed, and it cries itself out boldly in solidarity with the other mourners. The dead man comes out, and Jesus directs the witnesses, "Unbind him, and let him go" (John 11:44).

Katharine Drexel knew genuine sorrow. The deaths of Emma Bouvier Drexel and Francis Anthony Drexel were not unexpected griefs. Often, we expect our parents to go before us, and we expect these deaths to occur in old age as natural deaths. Such is not always the case. When twelve-year-old Katharine learned that her natural mother's death had occurred five weeks after childbirth, she was shocked, saddened to think that her own birth had brought about her mother's death. The mother that she knew, however, Emma Bouvier Drexel, had already been a powerful and loving presence in her life and continued to be so for many years to come. Years later, when Emma was dying, Katharine was able to comfort the comforter, but standing beside Emma's deathbed, she reflected on the helplessness we feel in the face of death. For all the Drexel fortune, Katharine could do nothing to counter the cancer against which Emma fought.

Again, when Katharine's father died two years later, Katharine ran for help, but human efforts proved futile. Katharine and her sisters Louise and Elizabeth were now left alone in the world, wealthy young women filled with a deep faith but also with many questions. What were they to do with their many gifts? It was not long before they found their answers in a loving service to others.

Soon, however, their work met with catastrophe. Elizabeth died in childbirth, and the baby died as well. Katharine was overwhelmed with grief. Over the course of her long life, Katharine Drexel witnessed the deaths of many of her loved ones. Again and again, she encountered the inevitability of death: her spiritual directors, her friends like Monsignor Joseph Stephan, her dear brothers-in-law, her sister Louise. Almost ninety-seven when she died, Katharine had experienced loss and its accompanying grief many times with the victories of death; yet she had also experienced many times the joy of having comfort in those relationships as her loved ones passed into their peace.

Katharine Drexel did not dwell in her griefs. Sadness was not a habit of mind. It was a genuine human experience, and she never denied herself the gift of tears that life offered her. She took her tears, however, into her prayers, where she found the transforming power of love. The Mother of Sorrows, with a sword piercing the heart, was an image that made sense to Mother Katharine. It had made sense to young Katie as well. She understood sorrow, but she also came to experience the divine fire of love that keeps us from dwelling eternally in the tomb of grief. If we go to Jesus with our grief, we will find someone who will be with us in it, someone who will continue to teach us how to pray in it and through it, and we will be moved to pray thankfully, confidently, even boldly in solidarity with others who share this love, whose hearts are in union with this divine fire.

To experience genuine sorrow is to live out one of the inevitable parts of life, but to dwell in it is to waste the gifts that are another important aspect of our lives. To dwell in sadness, to cultivate a habit of mind that is sad, is to miss out on the transforming power of the divine love that will go with us to the tomb, weep and sigh with us, but then remind us to lift up our eyes, give thanks and confidently let God do whatever it is that God is doing. We will find life, not death, freedom, not bondage.

The power of love will increase as we continue to turn away from sadness. We must not ignore genuine sorrow. We must weep when we must weep. After all, there is "a time to mourn, and a time to dance" (Ecclesiastes 3:4).


## REFLECTION QUESTIONS
Am I a joyful person? What have I done with the sorrows of my life? Do I console the sorrowful? Do I believe in the enkindling power of the divine fire of love? Have I experienced the enkindling power of this grace? Do I cultivate a habit of mind that is sad? Am I a witness of thanksgiving, of confidence, of love?

## DAY EIGHT

# Humility

## FOCUS POINT

Our pride tempts us to see ourselves as more important than we are and to expect more than others because of such self-importance. A healthy sense of humor may help us to remember our place in the greater scheme of things. Everything passes away. What really matters will ultimately be found in the eternal hands of God if we let the Spirit carry us.

*O Divine Spirit, I wish to be before You as a light feather, so that Your Breath may carry me where You will. [13P]*

*Keep me from sin in my weakness and despair. In each fall I shall run into Your arms as a child to its Father as dear Papa carried me into the ocean for an ocean bath. Your mercy, Your love is an ocean of love and mercy. [22–23P]*

*Humility is a help to acquire the perfection of every virtue; in fact, there is no virtue without it. [23R]*

*Oh, I am a lot of doctors now. [Duffy 366]*

H istory is filled with lessons about the downfall of the proud. Ancient stories remind us of the inevitability of such lessons. A mortal who attempts to steal fire from the gods finds himself chained to the top of a mountain. A great king who wants to be flattered by his daughters creates his own destruction and that of his dearest child. A woman who is obsessed with being "the fairest of them all" becomes a hag. Lady Macbeth's hands will never be free of the taint of what she has done. The history of the stories of humanity repeats some important lessons. Those who think they are in charge learn otherwise. Those who try to control others will eventually perish through their own machinations. The great Golden Palace of Nero is no more.

"All who exalt themselves will be humbled, and all who humble themselves will be exalted" (Matthew 23:12). The passage is a quintessential axiom even for some nonbelievers, though clearly many people, believers and nonbelievers alike, operate on an assumption of the opposite: the only way to get ahead is to push ahead of others. To stand back while others have the right-of-way might mean that others get to the finish line first, get the prize or choice piece of property, the better job, the higher salary, the desirable position for oneself or one's children. The highway to success is littered with the carcasses of the weak; at least, that is what the proud see. The proud do not want to find themselves victims in the competition, fools in the court, homeless in the storm, without fire when possession of fire seems possible, ruled by others when ruling over others seems so much more attractive, so much more comfortable, safer. After all, we live only once, so we might as well live like kings and queens, gods and goddesses.

Why would anyone be content to be a slave, to wait outside the store while everyone else is inside buying the best merchandise first, perhaps leaving nothing for the timid outside.

Often, those who are most uncomfortable with Jesus' words about humility are already caught up in the illusion that putting oneself ahead of everyone one else makes one stronger and that those who are foolish enough to be humble deserve what such weakness deserves: to be ridiculed, to be enslaved, to be considered nothing in the eyes of the world. Such fools put their sights on another world, one that doesn't exist. Such fools deserve their low position in life. If someone seems to disdain the world of the high and mighty, then let that person be crucified. At least, that view is the conclusion that the world seems to offer as its justification for its power-driven existence.

Such a view, however, is a distortion of the true nature of Christian humility. One of the common denominators of these stories of proud people from history, myth, and literature is the heaviness with which human nature seems to take itself. The more importance one attaches to oneself, the heavier the ego becomes. The overweight ego ceases to see itself as it really is. The wicked queen does not let herself see her own transformations in the mirror. The foolish king does not see how he has turned his good daughter out of his heart; he does not see until later when he himself has been turned out in the storm, homeless and mad.

Humility does not mean timidity. It might look like foolishness by others on the highway, but it may mean that the humble driver is the one who is safeguarding the family within one's own car rather than risking lives by insisting on speeding ahead of everyone else. People who see themselves as the most important person in the world are inevitably going to be in conflict with all of those others who also see themselves as Number One. The person to whom no one else is an equal is doomed to a hard lesson, unless that person destroys himself or herself before having to face the obvious. Everyone on the highway has a need to reach a destination. No one has an inherent right to be Number

One. Oedipus and his father fight over the right-of-way on a road. There are many ironies in that story, of course, but interestingly enough the conflict occurs at a point where three roads meet. Are the father and son eyeing the path ahead? Does it seem that there is only one possibility in the road and that someone else threatens to take it first? In this ancient story, the consequences of the conflict prove tragic.

Sometimes, however, the consequences do not seem tragic. We cut someone off in the road and laugh on our way to the party. There is no big deal in putting ourselves ahead of others. In fact, if we don't, someone else will. We justify our actions as sensible. There is only way one to get where I am going, and that is by making myself more important than those others clamoring at the door of the department-store sale.

What is seriously lacking in the stories of the proud is a healthy sense of humor. Oh, there is humor all right. These stories are often filled with ironies, sometimes grim, about the ways the proud become humbled. The cartoons from years ago caricature the enemy as a big buffoon, while the lovable, beleaguered roadrunner gets away. The kind of justice in children's stories is often shallow. It is intended to placate us, to make us laugh, or in the case of a bedtime story put us to sleep.

Genuine humility is a much tougher nut to crack. In one of her visions, the mystic Julian of Norwich saw the reality of everything reduced to the small, hard shape of a hazelnut. What is the essential quality of life that does not finally crumble? Surely those dictators who have erected their own statues have been proved wrong. Everything crumbles or is toppled. Every great dictator of the past has been tested by time and proved second rate.

The great Doctor of the Church Saint Teresa of Ávila reminds us, "All things pass away." Saint Katharine Drexel deeply understood this idea. In her long life, she saw many things pass away, many of her loved ones leave this world. Late in life, she found herself named to an honorary doctorate by Catholic University of America. She laughed and said, "Oh, I am a lot of doctors now." What did she mean by that? More likely than not, she was not claiming kinship with the great Doctors of the Church, whom she admired. Rather, she was admitting the many-faceted roles of her life, called as she was to be the source of healing for so many troubled people and so many troubled situations.

A young widow, rejected by a religious order because of its quick judgment that the young woman was running away from grief, wrote to Mother Katharine about possibly becoming a Sister of the Blessed Sacrament. Mother Katharine responded with a one-way ticket. The young woman entered Mother Katharine's order and lived a long, happy life as a religious. When a young Jesuit missionary, not knowing to whom he was writing other than a wealthy person who had money to give out, wrote to "Mr. M. K. Drexel" asking for money for his "Indians who love music," Mother Katharine responded immediately by sending a second-hand trumpet. Soon Father Jutz learned to whom he had written; thus began a correspondence that led to many other gifts for his people.

Katharine Drexel operated out of the principle of humility. There was once a visitor who came to see her, and the visitor approached a sister scrubbing the floor on her hands and knees. "Where can I find Mother Katharine Drexel?" the visitor asked, and Mother Katharine looked up from her work and identified herself.

A second-hand trumpet might be the best place to start. The floor was always a good place to work. Mother Katharine did not dwell in the clouds. In the ghettos of American cities, she worked and in fact contracted typhoid fever and pneumonia, almost dying later in New Mexico when the illnesses manifested themselves. We must do our work and appreciate the fact that not everything we do will bear fruit, but we must work humbly, letting the Spirit carry us wherever. Whatever keeps us from being as light as feather will hinder us from being carried by the will of the Holy Spirit.

In her meditations upon the Holy Spirit, she wrote, "The Holy

Spirit puts us in motion, lifts me up to the perfection of love. And here is the rejoicing of my soul: I am the Temple of the Holy Spirit…. The Holy Spirit lifts me up by the Spirit of love, and what does He require of me, but that I be humble and trustful" (9R).

She saw humility as an indispensable "help" toward every virtue. "In fact, there is no virtue without it," she wrote. Humility becomes a foundation then. It is not the end in itself. She lived the Gospel injunction, "All who exalt themselves will be humbled, and all who humble themselves will be exalted" (Matthew 23:12). Her life had set her on an exalted place. Her father's friends and associates were among the most illustrious of their day. Yet her father had warned his daughters not to marry a prince. Princes were destined for higher places in the world, and they might not have their sights upon higher values. Yet he and his wife wanted their daughters to enter society and take their rightful places. The three young women made their debuts into society, though Katharine makes only a slight mention of the event among her personal papers, as though it were not really an important event of her life.

Katharine knew the hardships of a fall. Literally, she fell once from a horse, breaking a collarbone. She had enjoyed horseback riding, and she learned its liabilities. Also, in other matters of life, it was possible to fall. Typical of the admissions of many saints, Katharine Drexel records her "weakness and despair." These admissions are not false modesty but the genuine expressions of self-understanding. She could see herself in the ocean of God's love because she had known what it was like to be carried into that ocean, first by a loving, human father and later and always by the God who bathed her in the "ocean of mercy and love."

Her humor was not the sarcasm of contemporary culture. There was no mockery in her laughter. If she laughed at herself, it was a laughter of self-understanding and of gentleness. Her self-understanding was no mere psychological trick to accommodate a sense of weakness against a prideful nature. It was a constant surrender to the God in whom she trusted, and the lighter her spirit became the more profound the movement of her heart in that relationship. She found herself carried into the ocean of mercy and love. She found herself light as a feather. Indeed, she is a doctor (though not proclaimed as such by the Church) whose prescriptions are timely. A dose of humility, increased daily over a lifetime, will make us light enough to be carried by the Spirit, honest enough to understand our place, and childlike enough to be carried into the ocean of mercy and love.

## REFLECTION QUESTIONS

Do I take myself too seriously? Do I not take humility seriously enough? When I fall, do I sulk in pride and self-importance that I am not stronger? Or am I willing to be as light as a feather and see my falls as opportunities to understand myself better in relationship to God? Do I live the Gospel injunction not to exalt myself? Do I see humility as a foundation for other virtues? When did I last experience God's ocean of mercy and love? Is humility a part of my experience of God? Do I pray for humility?

## DAY NINE

# The Cross

### FOCUS POINT

We are on a journey, trying to follow our Lord. The saints who have gone before us inspire us, but as models to imitate they sometimes remind us of how much we fail in our intentions. We want to be good followers, but the road to the cross is a journey of suffering, just as it is a journey toward suffering and into suffering and through suffering. No one wants to suffer, yet suffering is inevitable.

*Life is marked by suffering. The poor suffer, the great suffer. [27P]*

*Everything that is painful to the flesh, displeasing to the senses is a CROSS. Embrace all these little opportunities of suffering and you will be bearing the Cross of Christ, relieve the afflicted and He will accept it as given to Himself. [32P]*

*I did most earnestly pray in my Mass and at holy communion to implore grace to imitate Our Lord and to return Him love for love. I tried to offer Him what St. Margaret Mary desired—not to be left without suffering. I absolutely have not reached her desire. Naturally, I hate suffering. I did try, however. [30P]*

*The Passion was, by the very meaning of the word, something passive; it was accepted with active good will, but it was submitted to, not sought after as an instrument of self-torture. [5R]*

What do we see when we look at the cross? We have heard people say, "That was her cross in life" or "This is a cross you must bear" or "He had many crosses in life." The physical object of the cross has come to mean an experience or a set of experiences. History tells us that crucifixion was one of the most shameful ways to be executed, yet through the death of Jesus, it has become a sign of our redemption.

For many people, the Way of the Cross is an indispensable part of their Lenten experience. It would seem strange to celebrate this form of prayer during Advent. It has its place in the Church calendar, and it makes sense in its place. In life we cannot predict the season in which we will encounter a cross. We might be walking our very own *Via Dolorosa* while elsewhere a young couple is waiting for a child to be born. The poet W. H. Auden expresses this juxtaposition of lives in his poem "Museé des Beaux Arts." As Auden indicates in his poem, to understand suffering means more than to experience pain. There are many experiences for which we have no understanding. Two people can be trapped in the same elevator and emerge with radically different experiences. Even with their shared experience, which in reality might be viewed as an additional experience including their individual experiences, they might later explain the event in completely different terms and might feel completely different about their experience. The claustrophobic might have nightmares for months to come. The adventurer with a sense of humor might tell of the experience as one of the funniest experiences ever.

What might be a cross for some might not be for others. For some, to plan to fly across the ocean to visit a place one has always dreamed of might create excitement and anticipation of dreams come true. For others, the anticipation of flying across the ocean might create paralyzing anxiety and nightmares about death. What we have already experienced brings something to our anticipation as well as to our actual experiences of other things.

The artist Barnett Newman created a series of paintings entitled *The Stations of the Cross*. To some viewers, there is nothing on the canvases except streaks and splashes of white, black, and gray paint, with an occasional line of yellow or smear of red. To others, there is a progression from painting to painting through which one can journey, a *Via Dolorosa* without words, without human figures, without a narrative line in the way we expect stories of journeys to make sense. Once, in the National Gallery of Art in Washington, D.C., a woman entered the gallery space where the paintings were being exhibited. She glanced around the gallery and exclaimed, "There's nothing here. I could do this."

"Then why don't you," a man said. He had been intently following the series of paintings around the gallery.

The woman had already exited the gallery, but the man's challenge would have made no sense to her anyway. The woman had already decided that there was nothing here that she could not do, and if she had heard the man or been inclined to become engaged in conversation with him, she probably would have said, "I wouldn't do this if I could because it would be a waste of time. It doesn't make any sense."

The experience for the man was radically different from the woman's.

A series of paintings by Mark Rothko hangs in the Rothko Chapel in Houston, Texas. For some, the series of very dark paintings is nothing more than massive canvases of mostly black paint, with occasional splashes of dark purple. For others, the paintings are a tabula rasa upon which experiences with the paintings vary from visit to visit, depending on what is going on within the visitor at that particular time. For some, it is a chapel, a holy place. For others, it might be an interesting art space, but not a place to pray. For some, it is a bore and a waste of time. For some, it just doesn't make sense.

There are many people who look at a cross and say, "This doesn't make sense." All too often, we who see something else in the cross have to admit, "This just doesn't seem to make any sense."

We live in a culture that denies the redeeming possibilities of suffering. In our postmodern world, suffering seems inevitable but senseless. We believe in the power of medical prescriptions, or chemotherapy, or self-help miracles. For every pain known to the body or psyche, there will be a self-help book offering solutions. To many of us, acceptance of suffering sounds medieval. We might as well beat ourselves with whips or wear hair shirts. We believe in the painless surgery, the painless waiting room, the painless recovery. Even at funerals, we are now led away from the coffin while funeral-home attendants stand around waiting for us to leave before they actually place the remains into the grave or vault. At the funeral home, the family is left alone for the last intimate goodbyes, the doors closed to shield the sacred moment, but also to make sure that the rest of us do not see any great expressions of grief. Friends and other family members wait outside during the last moments while the funeral directors take care of the final details. The immediate family departs, and the casket is sealed. Yet much remains hidden from our eyes. Denial is part of our funeral customs today. We may not even remember from history that flowers and incense cover the smell of death. Today we make sure that we do not smell death.

Katharine Drexel wrote, "Everything that is painful to the flesh, displeasing to the senses is a CROSS." A bone spur in my foot is probably not what Saint Paul was talking about when he

referred to the thorn for the flesh given to him, "a messenger of
Satan to torment" him, to prevent him "from being too elated"
(2 Corinthians 12:7); yet a bone spur is painful to my flesh. Did
Katharine mean that everything that was painful to the flesh or
displeasing to the senses is a cross? An unpleasant odor from a
nearby industrial plant or loud music through my apartment wall
is certainly displeasing to my sense of smell or hearing, yet if I
had to live with such unpleasantries, they might indeed begin to
grate and grow in their power of annoyance. I might even grow
immune, no longer detecting the odor or perhaps subconsciously
blocking out the sound. On the other hand, a pain in a herniated
disc in my back might not be something that I could get used to.
No doubt the pain is in my back is a cross of greater magnitude
than the industrial odor or noise from my neighbor, yet Katharine
refers to all of these experiences as crosses, though she admits
that some are "little opportunities." Nevertheless, they are truly
opportunities to bear the cross of Christ if I bear them in the
spirit of our Lord. Jesus did not seek the cross. Jesus "accepted"
it "with active good will, but it was submitted to, not sought
after as an instrument of self-torture."

Katharine did not see the cross as the sign that God wants us
to suffer. She saw the cross as a sign of how we are to endure our
suffering. Suffering is unavoidable. How we suffer our crosses is
another matter entirely. We have to accept what we have no choice
about, but we can accept it with an "active good will." If we
must submit to something, then we must submit to it in the spirit
of our crucified Lord. On our cross, we might be tempted to curse
like one of the thieves on Golgotha, or under the weight of our
cross, we might fall repeatedly. Once we find ourselves in one of
life's uncontrollable situations, we may have no choice about what
happens to us. We do, however, have a choice about how to respond to such situations. If we follow the example of Jesus, the
passive state that we find ourselves in is not that of the disgruntled
victim but is "filled with the fullness of God," as we saw in the
chapter on loss.

What do we see when we look at the cross? A wall ornament? A piece of jewelry? An object of shame? A frightening symbol of something inevitable?

There are probably many more kinds of reactions to the cross than there are kinds of crosses that confront us. Before a wedding a little two-year-old flower girl saw the large crucifix in the sacristy. She reached up to touch the feet, which were within her reach, and not understanding the red paint that was splattered around the nail head, she began to sing, much to her mother's chagrin, "Jesus has happy feet." She was simply an innocent child who did not yet have any understanding of the cruelty of which human nature is capable. Katharine once wrote, "It is not because we are innocent that He comes; but rather to save that which is lost" (5R).

Older people looking at the cross bring to their perception their own experiences of pain and suffering. At a different wedding, a young groom once found himself mesmerized by the nails in the hands and feet of the corpus on the cross. He told some friends later that he could not take his eyes away from the sight of those nails. Needless to say, the friends were not surprised later when the marriage did not last.

A woman in mid-life once entered the house of a friend. The woman was in some of the most intense pain of her life. She wept, crying out her story with the friend and over the course of some time began to feel safe confiding even more of her pain to this friend. Later that year during Holy Week, the woman went to visit the friend. She was not in tears, though she continued to be in intense emotional pain. The friend had a small reproduction of a painting on display in his living room for the week. The woman gasped to see the image of the familiar sight: a man hanging on a cross. For the first time in the long crisis of the woman's pain, she had an insight about herself. "No one has ever done that to me," she said solemnly. It was almost as if she were seeing Christ for the first time, seeing past the dead Jesus hanging on the cross. The moment of insight was a turning point in the woman's life. It was not the end of her suffering. It was certainly not the end of her pain, but from that day forward, she had a powerful image in her heart of a way to accept the inevitable. It was the beginning of a period of peace for that woman.

There *are* people to whom such things have been done. We read about the crucifixion of some of the apostles. No one has ever done that to me, though perhaps there have been people who might have wished such a destruction upon me. Whole populations of people have suffered unimaginable atrocities, so unimaginable that there are people who would even deny that such things have happened.

Clifford Leech, writing about the nature of tragedy, tells us that "tragedy is the realization of the unthinkable." It is unthinkable that a man we know would kill his father and sleep with his mother. It is unthinkable that our next-door neighbor has cannibalized victims and saved their parts in his freezer. It is unthinkable that a woman would kill her children. Is it unthinkable that a husband or wife would be unfaithful, that an adult would seduce a child, that lamps might have human skin for their shades? Such things are hard to imagine, yet we know that they are within the realm of possibility. They may even have happened within our family, neighborhood, or country. When we face these situations and realize the cruelty and inhumanity of which we are capable, we might be tempted to decry the universe as a senseless place, a place where suffering is inevitable, unavoidable, and unredeemable.

But we live in a redeemable universe. Yes, these things can happen. They do happen.

Everyone on the spiritual journey discovers that no one is exempt from suffering. If suffering means an inevitable part of what we must go through (the Greek word from which it comes means "what we endure"), then suffering is an inextricable part of life. In the Garden of Gethsemane, Jesus prayed, "Abba, Father, for you all things are possible; remove this cup away from me; yet, not what I want, but what you want" (Mark 14:36).

Those of us who are trying to follow Jesus in our lives can find this Gospel passage comforting. Even Jesus prayed that the cup be taken away. It is natural enough to hate suffering. Only the masochistic would enjoy suffering, but to desire suffering is not to wish for an enjoyable experience. To desire suffering is to desire to move along the road which is indeed our life's road, to move toward that which we must endure, with the hope that wherever the road takes us will ultimately be in the hands of God, in the will of God. There are clearly things we must go through that we do not want to go through. There are certainly days we would rather skip, appointments we would rather cancel, conversations we would prefer not to have. When the circumstances of our lives present some inevitabilities, we may not be left with a choice to go through a particular event or experience. We may have to go through what we have to go through, yet how we go through it may become the hallmark of who we are.

In *Man's Search for Meaning*, Victor Frankl reiterates this idea a number of times. Confronted with torture by the Nazi SS, the prisoner Frankl realized that there was nothing that he could do to prevent what his captors would do to him. They could not, however, take away from him his choice of how to endure what he had to go through. What his captors did to him was their choice, but the disposition of his heart—before, during, and after torture—was his.

Who knows how any of us will react under pressure, under torture, faced with a cup we would rather not drink? It is comforting to have the perfect model of our Lord, praying in our natural inclination not to go through something that seems horrible, yet also praying that the perfect will of God be done in whatever we must go through. Yet the saints are sometimes frightening in their near perfection. How could Saint Margaret Mary actually desire not to be left without suffering. Such a desire seems unnatural and indeed impossible.

Katharine Drexel's response to such a saint's inclination of the heart has its comforting aspects for us as well. Here is one saint admitting how far she is from the holy disposition of another saint's heart. "I have absolutely not reached her desire," she wrote. "Naturally, I hate suffering." This second thought is no excuse, no rationalization. It is simply an admission of human nature. It is our human nature to hate suffering. What distinguishes some of us on the journey from others is, however, how we respond to it. Do we say, "Let me then go through what I must go through," or do we turn to cursing our captors or striking off the ear of the chief priest?

Katharine Drexel's conclusion is the admission, "I did try, however." She "did try" to follow the saint's desire not to be without suffering. There is a gentle self-acceptance in her failure. We can almost see the signs of a gentle smile on her face. Surely in Frankl's heart, there was great pain, but perhaps there was also a gentleness in his self-acceptance. If I have to endure this, then so be it. I will endure this, but afterwards, I will still know who I am and what I cherish and what is the substance of my hope. Moreover, my passage, my endurance, may actually tell me who I am on the journey in relationship to the God that I desire.

Saint Paul tells us that "faith is the assurance of things hoped for, the conviction of things not seen" (Hebrews 11:1). If we believe that there is a God greater than the momentary experience that we are faced with, then we can find strength in that surrender, an acceptance of whatever the road entails. Jesus' experiences in the garden and on the sorrowful path and on the cross itself are all parts of one greater experience, and if we believe that even Jesus did not know how all of these parts were going to fit together, then such cries as "Let this cup pass from me" and "My God, my God, why have you forsaken me" become rallying points between us poor pilgrims on the journey and our superlative example of what we are called to be, God's Word in the world. Our success pales in comparison to the saints, but we are not in competition with them or with God's Incarnation.

We are called to continue because we are not called to hang on our cross forever. We are called to endure because this road is ours, these crosses are our lives, and death awaits us at the end. We believe that something awaits us beyond what we must endure, though whatever it is must be put into the hands of God. We go through what we must go through. We endure, and we hope.


## REFLECTION QUESTIONS

What do I see when I look at the cross? What are the crosses that I have known? How have my crosses been part of my spiritual journey? Have I ever prayed that my cup be taken from me? Whenever the cup of suffering remains with me, what has been my attitude? Am I a person of hope?

## DAY TEN

# Thankfulness

### FOCUS POINT

To be thankful requires an effort, but it also requires a predisposition of our hearts. We believe that our God is a good God and that everything God sends us must be good since it is a gift from our good God. We have trouble accounting for evil, however. Surely, not everything in our lives can be good. If we are to thank God for our lives, how can we account for the evil around us, the evil that plagues us? It is sometimes easy to say "Thank you," but it is often difficult to be thankful.

*Thank God for everything that makes me die to self—die to sin. My whole life henceforth must be a conscious dying. Thank God for everything that makes me die, as now. [32P]*

*Arise from your Christmas thanksgiving to find your Jesus always with you, with you with His power and overshadowing you to make each action through Him divine. Arise from the Holy*

*Communion to find Him in the people, for whatsoever you do to
them, you do to Him, whatsoever you do to your Sisters you do
to Him. Arise to see in every single event in life God's Will, God's
Providence. [12R]*

*The Eucharist is the continuation of the Incarnation. [10R]*

———

We have all written thank-you notes, sometimes out of a
sense of obligation, sometimes out of our genuine expressions of thankfulness. How many times have we received a
thank-you note and fully believed the sentiment written within?
Why would we doubt someone else's sincerity? Perhaps we know
that our own words do not always convey a deeper attitude within
the heart.

Yet sometimes we deeply mean the words of our thanksgiving. Sometimes we are so overwhelmed by what we have received
that words do not seem able to convey the profundity of our
gratitude. We hear ourselves saying such things as "Words cannot convey..." or "I cannot begin to tell you how much...." We
might even sometimes find the need to thank someone for a thank-
you note when an expression seems greater than our gift.
Thankfulness can astound us with its magnitude, just as it can
embarrass us with its artificiality. "No, thank *you*," someone might
say, unable to let the last word rest in the air, unredirected.

"You're welcome" is an expression that seems to be losing
ground in our culture. Many of us have noticed the strange response we get when we say to someone who has just thanked us,
"You're welcome." It almost seems as if we have insulted people
sometimes. "What do you mean?" the person's face says. "I'm
*welcome*?"

"No, thank *you*."

The exchange becomes a kind of contest of words. Whoever
gets the last word is the person who can sigh relief. At last, I do

not have to thank you for thanking me for doing whatever it was that required a thank-you in the first place.

"What a terrible game it has become," a young bride lamented, facing hundreds upon hundreds of thank-you notes. Some brides have given up entirely, writing no thank-you notes at all. Others promise their mothers or friends that within a year of the wedding all of the thank-you notes will have been written. How often have we been surprised to receive a thank-you from a young couple not long after the honeymoon? We are surprised, perhaps delighted, if we do not occasionally wonder how in the world such people are able to take care of this responsibility so quickly. How cynical our reactions are sometimes. Is the early thank-you note genuine? Or is it merely the result of someone's obsessive compulsion? Even when we find prompt and clearly expressed gratitude, we might be tempted to doubt its motives. What can such an expression mean? Of course, the note says "Thank you," but what else does it say? What does it really mean?

We have become a cynical society. Thankfulness is only one of the objects of our cynicism. Perhaps if we examined our motives for saying "Thank you," we might learn much about ourselves.

The American statesman and former senator Eugene McCarthy once congratulated a host for a job well done but suggested that his host had thanked people too much. Take credit, he was saying, for what you yourself do. Perhaps we sometimes do not know how to be thankful for our own abilities and accomplishments. Not being thankful for our own strengths might mean that we lack self-awareness and do not fully utilize our capacities. Perhaps false modesty or pride keeps us from accepting someone else's generosity or gratitude.

A difficulty in learning to accept gifts from others as well as to accept our own gifts might indicate a problem with pride. Learning to receive everything else might also be a problem with pride. When good comes our way, we can readily admit that gratitude makes sense, even if we stubbornly resist being grateful; yet when bad comes our way, it is easier to resist. I do not deserve this bad that has come to me. Why should I be grateful for it? Early in the Book of Job, we hear Job telling his wife, "Shall we receive the good at the hand of God, and not receive the bad?" (Job 2:10). Receiving the bad goes completely against the grain. How can we accept the bad?

Paul's exhortation to the Thessalonians includes these words: "Rejoice always, pray without ceasing, give thanks in all circumstances; for this is the will of God in Christ Jesus for you" (1 Thessalonians 5:16–18). There are many circumstances in life which challenge our ability to give thanks. If I receive a frightening diagnosis from my doctor, should I be thankful? Perhaps eventually I might be grateful that the doctor has diagnosed my condition. Perhaps the diagnosis will save my life. What if it will not? Then perhaps I might eventually be grateful that I have learned the diagnosis so that I can get my affairs in order. These eventualities may help me, but it will be easier to be grateful when I reach them than it is now when I am trying to deal with the bad news.

Are there actually people who believe that there is no such thing as bad news? These people must be either fools, saints, or heretics. How can I say that the discovery of infanticide next door or in my own home is not bad news? What kind of insensitivity have I offered people when I fail to acknowledge the bad that has happened—or is happening—in their lives? Yet to tell people that they must give thanks to God for everything in all circumstances may be the sign of my own blindness and lack of compassion.

Paul is not alone in reminding us to thank God in all circumstances. Perhaps such encouragement is meant to inspire us or help us get through a dark time. All in all, however, thanking God for everything often seems beyond human capability. What does this injunction actually mean in our day-to-day lives?

Katharine Drexel tells us, "Thank God for everything that makes me die to self—die to sin. My whole life henceforth must be a conscious dying. Thank God for everything that makes me die, as now." When she learned of her sister's death, her first reaction was not gratitude. She had to struggle with her loss, just as she had to struggle so many times in her life with the loss of loved ones. After her genuine expressions of grief, however, she was able to pass into a state of peacefulness about the loss. She worked through her grief in prayer. Surely, her great love of the Eucharist was for her at the heart of this working-through process. For her, the Eucharist was "a continuation of the Incarnation."

Katharine Drexel loved the sacrament of gratitude—the Eucharist—so much that she first named her order the Sisters of the Blessed Sacrament for Indians and Colored People. In time, her sisters would adjust the name to meet the sensitive needs of what their foundress referred to as her "two beloved races." The name, nevertheless, indicates her love of the Eucharist and places it at the service of these people. As much as she loved eucharistic adoration, her writing reflects the direction of her prayer as it grew out of the thankfulness of her holy Communion. She tells her sisters to "arise" from their eucharistic celebration and let their thankfulness direct them threefold: (1) to arise finding Jesus within oneself and be transformed in the disposition of the heart and in consequent actions; (2) to arise finding Jesus in those with whom we come in contact so that everything we do for them we do also for our Lord; and (3) finally to arise finding God's will and providence in every event in our lives.

For Katharine Drexel, the life of thanksgiving expands then with every relationship—to oneself, to others, and to everything that happens in our lives. This exhortation comes appropriately in her meditations upon the Christmas eucharistic celebration, the prayer of thanksgiving for the feast of our Lord's nativity. "The Eucharist is the continuation of the Incarnation," she wrote. If we sincerely direct our thanksgiving to every aspect of life, how can we not find ourselves living out the Incarnation as it reveals itself in our lives, within us, within others, and within everything we encounter?

What is born in the cave of Bethlehem reveals the fullness of

God's love for us. Whatever must die in order for that fullness to grow must be part of God's divine plan. Whatever keeps me from living out the Incarnation—whether within myself or with others or in relationship to the events of our lives in the world—whatever is sin—that is what I must die to, and to die to sin is to let God work in me, in relationship to others and to the world.

Too often the word "thanksgiving" rings hollow. In the United States today, the holiday called Thanksgiving means turkey, cranberry sauce, pumpkin pie, and generally too much food. All day long there are parades and ball games on television. Granted, in many places on this special day, there are remarkable gestures of generosity: people working at homeless shelters, restaurant owners turning their establishments into one-day banquet halls for the poor and hungry, families gathering from far and wide to give thanks, congregations praying in solidarity for blessings received. What happens to these gestures on the following day? Pandemonium fills stores, and crowds fight their way through the retail frenzy. The idea of setting aside a day of Thanksgiving is no doubt a good idea, but the day has become for many just another obligation, a perfunctory thank-you note, something we have to do, perhaps even enjoy doing, but not a lasting state of mind. We re-enter our lives in the days after without much thought to our thankfulness. We have written the thank-you note, but we do not live a life of thankfulness.

Katharine Drexel knew the power of gratitude. She thanked God daily in her eucharistic celebrations. She thanked God daily for the gift of her life. She thanked God daily for the gift of God's presence in others. Even in her enemies she was able, because of her prayers of thanksgiving, to see the power of God's will. In an exhortation for eucharistic prayer, she urges us to "arise to see in every single event in life God's will, God's providence." God's will is not something against which we must fight. God's will, God's providence, is something for which to be grateful. Katharine believed in the Incarnation, and she lived her belief, finding God in the world around and within her.

## REFLECTION QUESTIONS

For what am I most thankful? Do I find something in every day for which to be thankful? What are the things that I have failed to be grateful for? Who are the people that I have taken for granted? What are the most difficult things in my life to be thankful for? Can I see them in the light of God's ultimate goodness? What keeps me from being a more thankful person? Do I make the effort to be thankful? How can I become a more thankful person?

## DAY ELEVEN

# The Quietest Way

### FOCUS POINT

As we mature in the spiritual life, we grow less interested in being the center of attention. As we shed the trappings of our ego, we come to experience the greater satisfaction of not being an object of adulation. As we grow in becoming more other-directed, we cease to be preoccupied with our inflated pride or our wounded ego. As we continue on our journey, we grow to appreciate the need to be quiet, both internally and externally. To grow in love, we must cultivate our quietness.

*The quietest way is the best. [23R]*

Jesus tells us, "Beware of practicing your piety before others in order to be seen by them; for then you have no reward from your Father in heaven. So whenever you give alms, do not sound a trumpet before you, as the hypocrites do in the synagogues and in the streets, so that they may be praised by others" (Matthew 6:1–2). When giving alms, we must remember not to have our works "trumpeted" or do what we do "to win human admiration." Again, Jesus warns us about the hypocrisy of not practicing what we preach. The scribes and Pharisees "do all their deeds to be seen by others; for they make their phylacteries broad and their fringes long. They love to have the place of honor at banquets and the best seats in the synagogues, and to be greeted with respect in the marketplaces, and to have people call them rabbi" (Matthew 23:5–6).

Katharine Drexel took these injunctions to heart. She wrote, "The quietest way is the best." She understood that "trumpeting" what we do is not in the spirit of the genuine Christian mission. Fanfare is noise, and noise is worse than a distraction. When I attract attention to myself, becoming in Paul's words a "clanging cymbal" (1 Corinthians 13:1), my work may lose its genuine character. It becomes an occasion of my pride, and I may completely forget the real reason for doing what I am doing. Little Katie learned early that the reason her mother fed the poor at the door was not to feel good about herself, not to get a tax break, not merely to negotiate an economic move or a psychological maneuver. Emma and her daughters fed the poor because the poor were hungry.

The quietest way does not always seem to be the best way to do a thing. As children, we learn to make noise to get what we want. The dynamic is powerful, and we learn that it works later in life just as well. The child learns in the quietness of a church or museum that an echo attracts attention and also learns that its parents will try to silence the loud voice of the child. Noise attracts attention. It has power. Demonstrators sometimes make noise to get attention. Sometimes, however, strikers know that their silent presence may be just as effective as loud voices. Noise is not always persuasive.

Sometimes the quietest way is a more effective way in accomplishing what we want. The stereotype of "strong silent type" suggests that not speaking may have advantages. The expression, however, is not "the strong quiet type." Quietude is not the same as silence. Being quiet, a person may look meek. Being silent, a person may look stupid. Both of these conclusions can be wrong, however. A quiet person may be more dangerous than a noisy demonstrator. The quiet child may be up to much more mischief than the brawling brat. We will look at silence in the next chapter, for it is clearly something other than the quietness to which Katharine Drexel was referring when she wrote, "The quietest way is the best." Certainly she never would have been able to build some of her schools if she had not understood the strength of quiet moves. Like her father, she knew how accomplish great things in the business world. Like her father, she understood the intricacies of negotiation, and she kept her focus on what she wanted to accomplish, not on drawing attention to herself and not on satisfying her own ego. The work was more important than accolades. She did not need the seat of honor at the banquet. Success was more important than applause.

At the formal dedication of Xavier University of Louisiana, Mother Katharine did not stand on the dais among the dignitaries. As the founder of the university, she surely should have had the first place of honor at such an event. Who could have been more important on that platform than the person who made the occasion possible? Yet Mother Katharine was nowhere to be seen. She watched the event from a nearby convent window. She was not interested in being the center of attention. She did, however, want to know that everything went well. She had already done the difficult work of establishing her university at a time when there was much opposition to education of her beloved black people. The point of her efforts was to ensure that they would be able to get the education that they needed and deserved. She was not interested in being congratulated on her accomplishments. She did not need to hear tributes to her generosity or to her other remarkable qualities that had fought prejudice and defied hatred and demonstrated her great capacity for love and justice.

We learn early in life how good it feels to be the center of attention. If we were the celebrant of childhood birthday parties, we no doubt enjoyed being the center of such attention. Everything is for me. The reason for the event is to commemorate the great day of my coming into the world. People come to my house. They bring me gifts. I get to open all of the gifts and to keep them, though I might concede letting my guests take home some small souvenir, some trinket, maybe even a piece of cake for a sick brother or sister. The party, however, is mine. I am the reason for it. I am Number One, for that day at least.

We have seen the pain of a young guest unable to understand that such a party may not focus on the guests. There is sometimes the child who tries to open gifts that are not his or hers or who tries to stand at the center of the group for the photograph, perhaps even trying to eclipse the birthday child. How many children's parties have been marred by the crying brat, the jealous guest who bursts the balloons unable to possess one of the birthday packages.

Childhood is filled with such evidence, and we are relieved, later in life, to be able to look back and laugh at our childhood ego. Yet adulthood has its own varieties of ego-centered events: competition on the job, infidelities in marriage and friendship, sour grapes in an assortment of candy-coated pills that we take to assuage our disappointments in life. I did not get the promotion or win the Citizen of the Year Award or get knighted to the bishop's honor guard. Sometimes we vicariously accept such awards, as when our child is elected class favorite or hits a home run or is selected Little Miss or is on the team that wins the trophy. Sometimes we go home angry because our child never got up to bat or didn't even make third place in a beauty competition. We hurt for our children, just as we had once hurt for ourselves.

The road to spiritual maturity has no room for sulking. It also cannot tolerate a parade of medal-wearing celebrities. There is reason for music and gifts at a celebration, but the reason is not to flatter my ego. There is a very good reason for music and gifts, and all of us present can make the music and share in the gifts.

There is, however, a greater reason for our celebration, and we have been invited to it, not to award ourselves for having made it through one more interval of our journey, young or old. We have been invited, and we need to celebrate and ought to celebrate. Not to celebrate is to waste another of life's great gifts. Mother Katharine celebrated the jubilee of her friend's ordination with a great feast and many guests. For her own anniversary, she wanted nothing. The direction of her attention and generosity was toward others. Celebrate? Yes, she no doubt had great joy in her heart on the day of the dedication of her university in New Orleans. Where was she? Not on the dais but at a distance, quietly watching, wearing no medals or crowns, holding no trophies, but indeed she was part of the celebration, a crucial part of it. Without her there would have been no celebration.

How often have we been part of a celebration but not quietly a part? How many times have our offerings of gifts been a display of our ego rather a genuine expression of our love and gratitude for having been invited as a guest of such a celebration? Do we want to sound our horn in the temple? Do we toot our own horn?

There are reasons to sound horns. We might need to give a warning. We might be making music. An important question in our spiritual journey must always be, "Who or what is at the center of what I am doing?" Is the noise in my life my ego calling out for attention, or does the quietness reflect my awareness that there is someone greater than me in this great celebration of life?

## REFLECTION QUESTIONS

When I give, do I give quietly? When I need to speak, do I speak quietly, or am I full of my own noise and ego? When I celebrate, how do I contribute to the celebration? Do I make joyful music, or do I merely contribute noise? Does the child in me sometimes sulk? Does the child in me sometimes rejoice? Can I accept being the center of my own birthday celebration? Can I accept being a guest at someone else's? Do I desire to become a person that is quiet?

## DAY TWELVE

# Silence

### FOCUS POINT

There is a time to be quiet. There is also a time to be silent. Sometimes our silence leaves room for ambiguity and confusion. Sometimes silence says more than words can ever say. When we are silent, we might be more eloquent than when we speak. We might be saying more. We might be loving more. When we are silent, we might also hear what we otherwise would never have heard. In silence we might discover how much more we are loved. Silence has its own rewards. Silence may not only be a means—it may also be a hallmark of our relationship to God.

*The silence of Jesus is powerful. [7R]*

*Imagine if this [Christ before Caiaphas] happened to me how I should feel. All around dark confusion, a roar. In such a case, I must be as Our Lord, serene and dignified. In the wee things He sends to His weak spouse how my impulse is to wrath. [7R]*

72

*Jarring discord is the mark of enemies. Peace and concord are the privilege of those who are on His side.... What did Our Lord do? He was silent. [7R]*

W hat does silence mean in my life? There are many kinds of silence. In contemporary life it is very difficult to find physical places of true silence. Is there really a silent forest where a tree falls and leaves us with the perhaps unanswerable question, "If no one is there to hear the sound, does the tree make a sound when it falls?" Perhaps such speculation means nothing in our lives. We know that, even if we wanted, we could not retreat to a place of perfect silence where there is no sound. If we go to our room to pray in silence, there are still sounds of the world around us: the buzz of a mosquito, the faint footsteps of a retreatant in a nearby room, the barely audible hum of transformers, or even the ringing of fluids in our own ear canals. Many people cannot tolerate the quasi-silence of a library with its scissor-like punctuations of crisp pages being turned or moist slapping sounds of gum being chewed between teeth. Saint Thérèse found the noise of a sister's rosary beads a distraction until she discovered in the sound the possibilities of prayer.

There are many kinds of silence. There is the proverbial "silence before the storm." There is also the silence after the tornado has passed. There is the silence at the center of a hurricane, and anyone who has survived a hurricane knows that the stillness in the eye of the hurricane is only a momentary state, that the storm has not passed but that there is still more fury coming.

The silence of a friend may be ambiguous. Does it mean that we are no longer in our friend's thoughts? Or does the silence mean that our friend is in trouble? Does our silence in answer to silence mean anything to the one we have found silent? Sometimes we can sit with a friend in silence and say more than in some of our long conversations. The old custom of sitting with the dead at night may have originally had some practical reasons, such as to make sure that the dead person was really dead and did not "wake" or to make sure that no one stole the body. In some cultures people speak to the dead in special ways at these wakes. The dead may be better able to hear or may seem closer to the divine, so people whisper their goodbyes to their beloved, or perhaps even whisper other words to the person who can no longer retaliate with words. Yet maybe we visit the dead because their silence speaks so powerfully to us.

The expression "the silence of the tomb" may sound like a cliché, but the silence of the tomb is an enduring silence. Hamlet's last words are "The rest is silence." No doubt Shakespeare was enjoying the double meaning of the word "rest." Hamlet will speak no more. His surviving friend Horatio will tell the rest of the story, but Hamlet is also on the brink of his own rest where silence is now possible. Earlier, confronted by the old fool Polonius in the library, Hamlet tells the old man, "Words, words, words." Hamlet is mocking the old man as well as pointing out the emptiness of so many words on the page. Too often our words signify little or nothing. Sometimes our silence is more powerful than our words.

There have many interpretations of the phenomenon of silence. Shusako Endo's great novel *Silence* deals with the Jesuit missionaries in Japan and their martyrdom. Our silence can signify our cowardice, or it can be the emblem of our bravery. Søren Kierkegaard names his persona in *Fear and Trembling* Johnnanes de Silentio, John of Silence. John of Silence tells us that silence is paradoxical. It contains both the divine and demonic. It can be a trap, but it can also be the point of understanding between us and the divine. Philosophers such as Max Picard in *The World of Silence* have analyzed silence as a phenomenon, and Bernard Dauenhauer investigated the subject in his book *Silence: The Phenomenon and Its Ontological Significance*. Students of Buddhism know that there are various forms of the Buddha's own silence. Non-Quakers are intrigued by what Quakers do not say in their silence. Some retreatants may struggle with thirty days of silence, whereas others afterwards may yearn for a life more filled with silence. For all such speculation and diverse experience, silence remains a mystery.

"Silence is golden," we have heard. Many of us have entered into the golden silence of a retreat. For some of us, silence is sometimes easy. It calls to us out of the noise of our lives, and we cannot get enough of it. For some of us, silence is sometimes frightening. We turn on the television as soon as we enter the house or perhaps leave it going so that it will be on when we return. As soon as we get into the car, we turn on the radio or CD player. Sometimes we surprise ourselves. The silent retreat turns out not to be golden and peaceful but filled with distractions or perhaps words that we had not expected. Sometimes the car radio or CD player is not what we want on the long stretch of road. Silence may be just what we want, to our surprise, or not what we want at all.

So we have also learned that silence is not always golden. The liability of clichés is that they can mean one thing at one time and then at another time mean the opposite. What do we mean when we say that silence is golden? The image that Katharine Drexel contemplated of Christ before Caiaphas is that of a powerful silence. All around our Lord was the roar of the world, the confusion of a world gone mad with its own power and arrogance. Jesus did not answer back loudly. He spoke when an answer was appropriate. He was silent when silence was the better answer.

In what way is silence a better answer, a stronger answer, than our words? Jesus knew that words were not going to stop his enemies. His enemies were looking for words to twist. Jesus allows them to ask and answer their own questions. "It is you who say it," Jesus says to the chief priest and then later to Pilate, and when faced with charges he "gave him no answer, not even to a single charge" (Matthew 27:14). In the Gospel of Mark, we read that it is to Jesus' silence that the high priest poses the second question, "Are you the Messiah, the Son of the Blessed One?"

to which Jesus answers with a response that leads the high priest to tear his robes and declare blasphemy (Mark 14:61–64).

To speak is sometimes to indite ourselves. It may mean an act of courage or an act of cowardice. To respond with words to an offensive story or joke might be an appropriate response. On the other hand, sometimes our silence is more powerful than words. Not to laugh at the joke that demonstrates racial hatred may say more to the teller of such a story or joke than any words we might utter. It certainly might have a deeper impact than anything we could say—sometimes yes, sometimes no.

As we know, there is a time to speak and a time to be silent. How do we know the mandate of any particular moment? Katharine Drexel finds "jarring discord...the mark of enemies." Perhaps if we would listen more carefully, we might hear what we need to hear and say what we need to say, rather than speaking out of haste or demanding we have the last word.

"Life is a tale, told by an idiot," Shakespeare wrote, "full of sound and fury, signifying nothing." These words belong to Shakespeare's tragic hero Macbeth, not a model for living the good life. William Faulkner borrows the term for one of his great novels, *The Sound and the Fury*. Like Shakespeare, Faulkner knew that there was a greater truth to be told than by a single character at a single moment. Macbeth's truth comes late in the play, a recognition of who he is and what he has done. Faulkner's novel sweeps back and forth through time, telling one great story through four different characters. It is the same story, yet it is not the same story. The teller, Benjy, the "idiot" of the Compson family, is the last to tell the story. His version is another of the gospels of the family saga. Matthew gives us one account, Mark another, Luke and John others. The truth is contained in all of the accounts. Faulkner concludes his novel with an additional history. About the family servant, Dilsey, and her people, Faulkner concludes, "They endured."

Likewise, we find the Acts of the Apostles, the enduring history that comes at what we might have thought was the end of the story, if we had not learned otherwise. The story is not yet over. We are still called to live it out, to endure, and as pilgrims on a spiritual journey, to continue on the road that will tell us who we are and what we have done and what we are doing. Who or what we will be is not yet known. Hamlet's beloved Ophelia says near the end of her all-too-brief life, "Lord, we know what we are, but not what we may be."

Do we know who we are? Do we know who Jesus is? Who do we say that he is? Caiaphas, Herod, and Pilate each had a chance to ask. Each had a chance to answer. In these encounters, do we identify with the interrogator, fuming at the silence of our enemy? Or do we respond like Jesus, with words when words are appropriate, with silence when silence says more?

## REFLECTION QUESTIONS

Do I cultivate silence in my life? How often has my silence been the mark of cowardice? How often has my silence been the mark of my peacefulness and concord? How often have I spoken merely to get the last word, to assert my own sound and fury, when in reality I have asserted nothing? Are there particular places in my environment that are more conducive to silence than others? Can I find silence even in places that are not conducive to the silence that I need? Do I have access to the silent chambers of my heart? Do I let God have access to these chambers?

# DAY THIRTEEN

# Prayer

## FOCUS POINT

There are many ways to pray. In praying the Our Father, Jesus taught us how to pray, but as we continue to grow in the spiritual journey, Jesus continues to teach us. If our learning how to pray is a process, there can be no end to the process so long as we are alive. Our relationship to the human and to the divine will always be part of our prayer until we reach our life's last "Amen."

*It is not we alone who pray, nor do we pray by our own strength; nor is it our own indigence we have to give. It is Jesus who prays in us. It is by His infinite merits that we pray, it is of His infinite treasure, His inexhaustible satisfaction. [16R]*

*Prayer can reach where the pen fails to go. He who is faithful in prayer will serve God with fervor. [18P]*

*Lord, help me love you in the way you deserve to be loved. [V]*

---

W hat part of our lives consists of conscious, intentional
prayer? Many people have had the experience of prayer
in recognizable and identifiable ways. As children we might have
had an early experience of grace before meals or night prayers led
by a parent. As we grew older, we might have learned to recite
certain prayers such as the Our Father or the Hail Mary or the
Act of Contrition. We might have grown up in a tradition that
used the Bible as instruction in Sunday School, or we might have
gone to prayer meetings in an evangelical church. We might have
experienced silence during Holy Week or at a Quaker meeting.
We might have heard or experienced speaking in tongues at a
Pentecostal prayer meeting or at a large charismatic conference.
We might have been prayed over by a minister in a hospital or
been prayed for by a friend whose beliefs seemed radically different from ours. The experience of prayer is as vast as the differences
among people. No one's experience can be identical to someone
else's, yet there are some fundamental characteristics that many
of our prayer lives have in common.

In fact, there are people who would deny that they have any
conscious prayer life yet nevertheless have described personal
experiences that reveal some of these fundamental characteristics. A high school student once described his experiences in a
duck blind on a cold winter morning and in a fishing boat on a
still pond on a summer day as experiences that had the power to
change his life. Being alone in nature was for this young man a
rare opportunity for him to filter out the noise of his life and be
still. He said that in that stillness he was able to be more in focus
than at any other time in his life. Something happened to him in
those experiences that was unlike anything else he knew. He could
not put the experience into words, but he knew that he felt changed
by those times in nature. Later, back at school or at his after-

school job, he sometimes yearned to be back in the duck blind or in the fishing boat. Escapism? Perhaps for many such experiences might be merely an escape and no more a religious experience than the mindlessness of a video game or a drug-induced stupor.

For some, playing a musical instrument might be prayer; for others, it might be a display of the ego. For some, a Zen retreat might be a turning point in their prayer life; for others, it might a frustrating experience never to be attempted again. For some, writing is a chore; for others, a compelling craft or a challenging but satisfying part of their work. For some, writing is prayer; for others, it is not. Saint Benedict teaches us that to work is to pray. Many people have a hard time seeing their work as prayer; others do not.

This chapter in no way attempts to give a definitive statement about the nature of prayer. Nor is it meant to be a comprehensive analysis of prayer as found in the writings of Katharine Drexel. The intention of this book is to meditate upon some of the wisdom left to us by Saint Katharine Drexel that was the fruit of her prayer life. For those who might wish to study Saint Katharine Drexel's actual written prayers in greater depth, readers are urged to look at the little book *Praying With Mother Katharine Drexel: Taken From Her Writings* (Mother Katharine Drexel Guild, 1986), which contains a wide variety of such prayers that she wrote out and left behind. Clearly, her prayer life could not be summed up on paper, but she did leave us numerous meditations. Granted, some of these were for her own use, and she wrote out meditations at times as part of her prayer life. Some of these were meant to be shared with members of her community. Others we have because writing for her was sometimes part of her prayer life— sometimes, but certainly not always and most probably not even most of the time.

Nevertheless, regarding Katharine Drexel's ideas about prayer, here are three observations useful for our consideration at this point: (1) We are not alone when we pray. "It is Jesus who prays in us." (2) Prayer changes our lives and the lives of others. "It can reach where the pen fails to go." (3) Fidelity in prayer is related to our service to God.

If we want to pray or if we want to improve our prayer life, we might ask the question, "How are we to pray?" For those of us who follow Jesus, we have a model. The Gospel of Luke reports, "He was praying in a certain place, and after he had finished, one of his disciples said to him, 'Lord, teach us to pray, as John taught his disciples,'" and Jesus answers with the Our Father (Luke 11:1–4). In both the Gospel of Matthew and the Gospel of Luke, we find Jesus continuing to speak about various aspects of prayer. In Matthew, for example, we soon thereafter find the famous passage that reassures us not to worry: "So do not worry about tomorrow, for tomorrow will bring worries of its own. Today's trouble is enough for today" (6:34). In Luke, we hear the story of the persistent friend at the door, and we are reminded of the need for perseverance in prayer: "So I say to you, Ask and it will be given you; search, and you will find; knock, and the door will be opened for you. For everyone who asks receives, and everyone who searches finds, and for everyone who knocks, the door will be opened" (11:9–10). Meditations on these two passages alone give us much fuel for thought, and no one can exhaust the possibilities of meditating upon the Our Father.

Katharine Drexel wrote, "It is not we alone who pray, nor do we pray by our own strength; nor is it our own indigence we have to give. It is Jesus who prays in us. It is by His infinite merits that we pray, it is of His infinite treasure, His inexhaustible satisfaction." If Jesus is praying in us, we are never alone in our prayer, and we can never cease growing in our relationship with God because of the infinite treasure that is praying in us.

Secondly, prayer changes our lives and the lives of others. We have heard the expression "The pen is mightier than the sword." We know that the sword can change history. So too can the pen, yet Katharine Drexel tells us that prayer can reach "where the pen fails to go." She experienced the power of prayer in her personal life as well as in the public life of her ministry. We can be sure that the great prayer life she experienced was vast and complex in its richness and diversity and that she often saw the fruits of her prayer. Yet often we do not see the fruits of our prayer. The object of prayer is often not to gain something or to make something happen. Prayer is not magic. If we attempt to use it merely to gain something or to make something happen, we are probably missing the point of prayer. Does my prayer give praise to God? Is my prayer an expression of my thankfulness? Is my prayer life consonant with the way I live and with the way I work? If I listen to Jesus praying within me and if my heart responds, then I will find the power of prayer radiating in my life. I will come to see that prayer and the changes in my life go hand in hand, even when the changes may not be the changes that I thought I had wanted.

Thirdly, she tells us that fidelity in prayer is related to our service to God. The person "who is faithful in prayer will serve God with fervor." There will be a correlation between our faithfulness in prayer and the fervor of our service. Our perseverance fuels our fervor. Infidelity or lack of commitment in our prayer life will be matched by a lack of fervor in how we live out our calling to serve God.

Of the known stories about Saint Katharine Drexel's prayer life, perhaps none is more endearing than one that resulted from something overheard. One night as Mother Katharine was praying, a sister entered the chapel to pray. Not wishing to disturb the foundress at prayer, the sister had quietly begun her own prayer when she heard Mother Katharine pray aloud, "Lord, help me love you in the way you deserve to be loved."

It was no doubt an awesome moment for the sister. She had entered someone else's sacred space unheard, undetected, and had witnessed an intimate conversation between the saint and her beloved. The sister had heard the saint's prayer. She could only conclude that the saint had heard the beloved's answer.

Many times in Mother Katharine's long life, people witnessed the external gifts of the saint's prayer life. Katharine herself as a young child had witnessed the external manifestations of her parents' prayer life. The family home contained a private chapel. Her father prayed daily at home before going to work at the bank with his partner Mr. Morgan. When her mother Emma died, Katharine saw her father go into a room in the home and close the door behind him. She knew that her father was praying out his grief for the loss of his wife. She knew that when her father played the organ in the family home, he was also playing out his prayer into music. She knew that there were many ways to pray. She had visited Rome and prayed at the tomb of her patron Saint Catherine of Siena in the Church of Santa Maria Sopra Minerva. She had visited France and Germany and Pine Ridge, South Dakota, and heard the diverse languages of the world. She was dedicated to traditional ways of praying like the rosary and the Liturgy of the Hours, and prayer before the tabernacle was an essential part of her life, yet she knew that her work among the poor in cities' ghettoes was also prayer, and she urged her sisters to get up from their Christmas eucharistic celebrations and thanksgiving and go out to love and serve others.

During the three years of her mother's struggle against terminal cancer, young Katharine had considered the possibility that she might have a vocation to the contemplative life. Perhaps she was called to spend her life away from the world in cloistered prayer. After her father's death, she eventually found her true vocation, not as a cloistered nun, not as a Philadelphia socialite-wife, but as a missionary sister. Even when she was confronted with the possibility of founding a missionary order, she pulled away at first, only to discover in prayerful discernment with a wise spiritual director that she was indeed called to such a public missionary life. Only much later in life—in her seventies—did a heart attack force her into confinement and eventually make possible the twenty years of contemplative life that she would enjoy at the end of her life in the motherhouse.

Thomas Merton writes about "contemplation in action" in

his book bearing those words. Mother Katharine lived out those words in the first seventy-five years or so of her life, and at the end she experienced the other side of that prayer, contemplation in place, so to speak. Yet her presence in the community manifested itself just as powerfully as it had when she was in action in the outside world. Young novices would see her wheeled in the makeshift wheelchair into the tribune overlooking the chapel and would know that she was praying with them and for them. From time to time she would write with one of her saved, short pencils on scraps of paper. These notes were occasions of her meditations, a technique related to her lifelong journal-keeping. Even as early as in her childhood journals, she had recorded facets of her prayer, words that indicated her intentions, words coming out of her deepest desires.

Only her beloved would understand the reciprocity of this love relationship. Witnesses might see their foundress in prayer or overhear an occasional utterance or later read the notes on the scraps of paper left behind, but no one could doubt that the fullness of Katharine Drexel's prayer life was richer than any witness could observe. It was obvious to all who knew or observed her that she had a great capacity to be focused on her beloved, no matter how she lived out that desire and that love. Her missionary work indicates her realization of the inequality that is inherent in relationships, whether it is our relationship with the divine or our relationship with other human beings. Her prayers continued to reveal to her the infinite goodness of her God that we can never be a match for. God will always deserve more love than we can express, yet the more we open ourselves to this love, the more we will be able to experience it with God and with others because love begets love.

She understood the human and she celebrated it. She yearned for the divine, and she celebrated it as well. There was no division in her beloved. Jesus was both human and divine. She accepted the great mysteries of her faith and celebrated them in her public and private life. In truth, for most of her life, there seemed to be no division between her public and private prayer life. When she rummaged through her community's kitchen garbage for pieces of bread to salvage for herself in order not to waste food, she was acting not out of an expression to make a public statement, but merely out of the direction of what her heart was telling her. When she saved short pencils and sat in the makeshift wheelchair, she was not making a public show of her poverty, she was simply living it out as one of the fruits of her prayer. What she did in life made sense because of what went on within her prayer life.

## REFLECTION QUESTIONS

What are the ways that I sometimes get stuck in my prayer life? How can the traditional ways that I have prayed in the past still be fountains of grace for me? What obstacles interfere with my dialogue in prayer? Do I listen attentively to what God is saying to me in prayer? What have I been saying to God? What have I not been saying? Am I open to new ways of praying? Do I see my work as prayer? Do I see my relationships with people as invitations to grow in love?

## DAY FOURTEEN

# Love

## FOCUS POINT

There are many kinds of love. The word *love* itself may be one of the most abused words in our vocabulary. Some people use the word too much and too lightly. Others may not use the word often enough. Still others may not use the word at all but demonstrate love in all manner of ways. One thing is certain. Love is not a thing, though love is a gift. If love is defined as a thing, it must be understood as a relationship. Who or what we love tells much about us, and the nature of our love affects our relationships with everyone and everything in our lives.

*Love is a gift, a gift I earnestly beg for each one of you, so dearly loved by our Lord.... Let us pray for each other very earnestly this Christmas and beg the Infant Jesus with great entreaty to increase our love. [UAR, Christmas letter to the Sisters of the Blessed Sacrament, 1920]*

*My beloved to me and I to Him. [11P and 23P]*

*Love wants joint ownership of property. It wants to share fortune and misfortune. It is in the nature of love—its instinct to give everything with joy and happiness. [11R]*

When we search history for what we call great love stories, we often find that the direction of great love stories is toward tragic endings. Only in fairy tales can we count on the lovers living happily ever after. That is not to say that there are not love stories with happy endings or with happy protagonists. The opposite, however, is what we often find. *Romeo and Juliet* is a great love story; the story of Cinderella is not.

In the novel *The End of the Affair* by Graham Green, a woman and a man move in different directions. Long after the affair is over, the man discovers the reason for the woman's decision to end the affair. She is struggling with a promise to God in thanksgiving for her lover's having been spared in a bombing raid. The novel does not oversimplify her choice: We are not caught between loving God versus loving another human. What happens in the relationship is that the woman finds herself drawn to a greater capacity to love than she had previously experienced and also to a greater love for both the human and the divine. For her, though, there is a physical separation, she does not cease loving the man; in fact, her love both for him and for God grows and ultimately becomes that healing kind of love that begets more love. For the man in this novel, however, things are different. He does not grow with her in love. He grows in bitterness and confusion. Their capacity to love reflects the different directions of their lives. They do not see love in the same light. They cannot travel together in the same direction.

Popular songs reveal the myriad definitions we have for love: "Love Is a Many-Splendored Thing," "What a Fool I Was for

Love," "Ah, Sweet Mystery of Life at Last I've Found Thee," "I Love Paris in the Springtime." The examples seem endless. Raymond Carver has a short story "What We Talk about When We Talk about Love," which is also the title story of one of his collections. "What Is This Thing Called Love?" asks the title of another song. It is a good question. Is love indeed a "thing" at all?

Generations ago teachers reprimanded children who used the word to refer to their feelings for things. "You cannot love candy," the teacher would say. "You can only love people." Yet children and adults alike use the word widely today to mean strong feelings for people, places, things, and experiences. "Don't you just love this weather?" or "I just love that color on you" or "I love New York." Teenagers (as well as people well beyond their teen-age years) have uttered the cry, "I'm in love again," only to fall out of love with a change of a season.

Generation after generation, people have tried to define love. Shakespeare considers a definition in his Sonnet 116, which begins, "Let me not to the marriage of true minds / Admit impediments. Love is not love / Which alters when it alteration finds / Or bends with the remover to remove." He idealizes love as a constant, something that does not change. How many people who have claimed to be "in love" will claim that love never changes? Perhaps it is only one of the two people that changes, not love. Perhaps it is both of the people involved in the relationship that change. Perhaps love is, as the sonnet claims, "an ever fixéd mark that looks / On tempests and is never shaken." Yet often in tempestuous relationships what was thought to be love dissolves in the storm, and the two people separate, no longer "in love" at all.

When we look at relationships that endure, examples of what must be genuine love, we ask ourselves what it is that makes some relationships strong enough to endure the ravages of time. A man and a woman live together happily for seventy-five years of marriage. Their predisposition to live so long may be genetic, but what is the secret of such a long-lasting and happy relationship? People might give all kinds of answers, but ultimately we have to admit that such longevity in love relationships is rare. What accounts for the enduring qualities of a loving relationship?

A woman whose grandparents had lived such a life experienced such a loving marriage herself, though her husband died before their thirtieth wedding anniversary. The woman readily admitted that she had not inherited any special "happy love gene" from her own parents, both of whom had been good, loving people but whose marriage was not one of those great love stories in life. The woman grieved when her husband died and never remarried and never wanted to remarry. Even thirty years after her husband's death, she would still speak of him as though he were a living relationship. Her love had not altered, though her beloved had been taken away. Many people might say that she had idealized her dead husband, but the truth was that she had had one of those great loving marriages, like her grandparents' marriage. She readily acknowledged that what she had experienced was rare, and she remained grateful for the relationship, which was in her past but for her was also still part of her enduring life.

Many years after her husband's death, one of her grown children asked her, "What is love?" Without hesitation, she began, "Love is something which requires work. It takes two people, and it is not easy."

Katharine Drexel described love as a gift.

The woman's child asked her, "Would you say love is a gift?"

Again, the woman did not hesitate to answer. "Yes, love is a gift. It is not a present. It is not a thing. It *is* a gift, but it is something that requires effort. You have to work at it."

Love as a gift might be seen as the mutual gift of the two people in the relationship. Both have to give. In a human relationship, the gifts are subject to our human limitations, so love requires our efforts to give of ourselves sometimes when we do not feel like giving, to be patient when we do not feel like being patient, to listen even when we are tired, to be silent when our beloved needs silence, to be still when stillness is the need, to move—even to move far away—when a move is necessary, to

confront when confrontation is required. Any child can see this
in his or her parents' marriage, no matter how happy or unhappy
the marriage. There are times in human relationships that effort
is necessary, and many relationships dissolve because people are
not willing—or in some cases unable—to do what is needed. Sometimes they simply cannot *be* what seems to be needed.

Our relationship with the divine cannot be divorced from our
relationships with one another. "Those who say, 'I love God,'
and hate their brothers or sisters, are liars; for those who do not
love a brother or sister whom they have seen, cannot love God
whom they have not seen" (1 John 4:20). We are called to love
one another, and that love will then be consonant with our love
for God. It will then also *be* our love for God.

Yes, it takes effort to love God, just as it takes effort to love a
human being. Does it take effort to be loved by God? Clearly,
once the human limitations are removed from the "other," the
relationship ought to be an easier one. God has no limitations,
that is, no human frailties. Yet many people on the spiritual path
speak of their difficulties in their relationship with God. For them,
the relationship is not easy. It takes effort. It might be a gift from
God, but it is not easy being in such a relationship, especially
when the "other" is perfect. Or is it not easy to be loved?

For Katharine Drexel, the relationship with her beloved was
two-way: "My beloved to me and I to Him." The philosopher
Martin Buber meditated long of the reciprocity of love in the great
book *I and Thou*. The movement toward another involves the
recognition of the other's awareness of me. It is the very nature of
this relationship, writes Katharine Drexel, to want "to give everything with joy and happiness." Traditional wedding vows list
daring polarities for those wanting to share everything, "richer
or poorer," "in sickness or in health," to share fortune and misfortune. For loving people such vows are easy to say because it is
the very nature of love to want to share everything.

Why is it then that people reach points in their lives of no
longer wanting to share? Divorce settlements are not always easy

agreements. Sometimes, one person wants this piece of property, and the other person is glad to relinquish it, no longer wanting a part of something that the other cherishes. Or perhaps both people want the same piece of property and so find themselves fighting over the division of it, neither of them wanting the other to have any part of it.

Katharine Drexel had no prenuptial agreement with her beloved. There were no conditions attached to commitment other than to love. Out of her desire to grow in love, she continued to keep herself open to love, always with the commitment of her heart to deny her beloved nothing, to give everything that she could give. Like the great prayer of Saint Ignatius of Loyola, she embraced her beloved with the prayer, "Take, Lord, and receive all I have and possess." The more she shared with her beloved, the more she wanted to give.

Perhaps her parents' love had engendered this inclination. Her father's will, after all, had conditions attached to it which said that finally everything would go to charity. After his three daughters were provided for, after all of his direct descendants were provided for, everything would go to the charities specified to receive the first fruits, the first ten percent of his estate; that is precisely what happened when Mother Katharine died at the age of ninety-seven: the entire trust went to charity. Francis Anthony Drexel and Emma Bouvier Drexel provided for their children because they wanted to share everything they had with their children, including their love of the poor, including their devotion to those less fortunate. The Drexels gave their daughters great love and instilled in them a great willingness to give what they had for those who did not have. Katharine and her sisters learned early in their lives the joy of sharing one's fortune.

It was only later in their lives that they would learn the gift of sharing misfortunes with others. When Elizabeth died due to complications of the childbirth that also took the life of the child, Katharine wept. Again, years later, when her sister Louise died, Mother Katharine cried, "Oh, my God, my God. I cannot believe that life is taken from me. Oh I cannot believe it…Wait…Wait…I must…Oh, my God, my God, I cannot…I cannot. It is not that I want anything different from what God wants…I cannot believe it" (Duffy 375). The biographer Sister Consuela Duffy reports that "as the day wore on composure came and complete submission to the Will of God. The calm expression on her face was evidence of the triumph of grace."

Katharine was the last of her immediate family. She had survived them all, and she had reached the painful point of no longer having any of those beloved family members with whom she had shared so much. Those people who visited her later on that day when Louise had died saw the calmness that love was once again bringing into her life. Because of her relationship with her beloved, she was able to give everything with joy and happiness, even to give up her beloved sister and the last member of her family to her beloved when that was what was asked of her. She heard the words of her beloved and lived them.

Jesus tells us, "Just as I have loved you, you also should love one another" (John 13:34). It is a mighty challenge, but it is one that once set in motion continues to beget more love.


## REFLECTION QUESTION

Do I use the word *love* lightly? Do I really distinguish between genuine love and other powerful feelings of desire? Whom have I loved in my life? What is my relationship to things? How have I shared ownership with others? What are my fortunes? How have I shared them with those I love? How have I shared misfortunes? When I give, do I give everything with joy and happiness? Am I a loving person? What prevents me from being a more loving person? How am I called to become a more loving person?

## DAY FIFTEEN

# Peace

### FOCUS POINT

We yearn for peace. Amid the problems of our lives, we face many demands. There is always something to do. Sometimes there is much to do, sometimes too much. We never seem to have enough time. We schedule appointments and live by calendars and alarm clocks, rushing toward and against deadlines. Perhaps we sometimes have too much time on our hands, and we don't know how to manage it. We may become bored or restless. Either extreme can be exhausting. Either extreme may signal trouble in our spiritual life. What is the best way to do what we need to do? There is a time for everything. Unless we find the balance that we need, we will not be able to live the present as we meet it; all in all, there is no better way to meet it than with peacefulness. What is peace? In the world, peace often seems a fragile thing, but Jesus promises us a peace that is not fragile.

*Peacefully do at each moment what at the moment needs to be done. [23R]*

---

W hat needs to be done? Funeral after funeral, we have heard the reading from the third chapter of Ecclesiastes that reminds us that for everything there is a season. Perhaps sitting in the pew is the workaholic, squirming to be reminded that not everything can be finished. Nearby may be sitting the procrastinator, hand over mouth, swallowing more guilt about the things not yet done. If the workaholic is restless trying to finish the future ahead of schedule, the procrastinator is tormented by an inability to finish the past. Neither of these two knows how to live out the Gospel injunctions about the day at hand: today. Both of them are too busy looking at their watches or appointment books to see the birds of the air or the flowers of the field to which Jesus refers. "Therefore do not worry.... But strive first for the kingdom of God and his righteousness, and all these things will be given to you as well. So do not worry about tomorrow, for tomorrow will bring worries of its own. Today's trouble is enough for today" (Matthew 6:31, 33–34).

To be present to the here-and-now does not necessarily mean to "seize the day," the age-old *carpe diem* theme of "Eat, drink, and be merry, for tomorrow we die." Saul Bellow's great little novel entitled *Seize the Day* gives readers a tormented soul who does not know how to meet his own needs or how to live the holiness of every moment. Struggling against his own ruined past and his dismal future, Tommy Wilhelm listens to the ravings of an articulate con artist, who urges him to live in the present moment. But there is an important difference between seizing the day and living it fully. At the end of Bellow's novel, Wilhelm finds himself sitting in a pew at a stranger's funeral, wailing, unknown by those around him. He is sobbing to have "sunk deeper than sorrow," to have come closer to his "heart's ultimate need."

What is our heart's ultimate need? How do some of our needs differ from others? What are our needs, and what is it that needs to be done today? "O, reason not the need," Shakespeare's King Lear laments when his two unloving daughters rationalize away all of the things which he thinks he needs. It is only too late in life, when Lear discovers the terrible things that he has done to his faithful and loving daughter, that he discovers truly who he is and what he has done.

As we grow older in the spiritual life, we come face to face with the exigencies of time. Once we have simplified our needs, whether voluntarily or involuntarily, we are left with the choice of how to meet the remaining challenges of our lives. How are we to meet these challenges? To the young and old alike, Katharine Drexel would answer, "Peacefully."

How many of us meet the conditions of our lives but either accept grudgingly or fight in denial or anger? Once we are resolved to do something, how we do it makes all the difference. A friend offers to do something for us, but we realize that the friend has offered out of a sense of obligation and may even be impatient with us when we do not allow him or her to do it in a particular way. Often what we do has little or nothing to do with peacefulness. We do what we do because we are somehow constrained, forced, and though we do it, we do it with a hard heart, perhaps even too quickly in order to get through it, or laboriously and too slowly because we force ourselves into a perfectionism that is marked by our ego, not by our peacefulness.

What does it mean to do something peacefully?

When we look at history, we find that peace seems to be a very fragile thing. Where is Augustus Caesar's Pax Romana today? Often in war there seems to be a time of peace established, only to have it crumble with old animosities rekindled. The history of violated treaties demonstrates the tentativeness of such proclamations of peace. Often in the midst of celebration for so-called victories of peace, we have found new insurrections and violence born, old stories and animosities continuing. There have been periods of peace in history, but they have always been followed by periods of war and turbulence.

Jesus said, "Peace I leave with you; my peace I give to you. I do not give to you as the world gives. Do not let your hearts be troubled, and do not let them be afraid" (John 14:27). The Prince of Peace is not a prince of this world. The peace that Jesus gives is not the fragile or tentative peace that worldly princes achieve. Yet are we not to try to achieve peace in this world? If so, how are we to achieve it? Apparently, it has already been given to us. Why don't we have it?

Jesus also tells us, "So when you are offering your gift at the altar, if you remember that your brother or sister has something against you, leave your gift there before the altar and go; first be reconciled to your brother or sister, and then come and offer your gift. Come to terms quickly with your accuser while you are on the way to court with him, or your accuser may hand you over to the judge, and the judge to the guard, and you will be thrown in prison. Truly I tell you, you will never get out until you have paid the last penny" (Matthew 5:23–26). Until we have resolved the conflict with our brother or sister, we cannot proceed with offering our gift at the altar. It will make no sense. The conflict will interfere. In terms of the law, we will find ourselves in a downward spiral into imprisonment until we have "paid the penny," and how will we be able to pay the penny once we have lost our freedom? Not to resolve our conflicts keeps us from moving forward in spiritual ways as well as in worldly ways.

The peace that Jesus gives us is not the fragile peace of the world. It does not depend upon the limited conditions of two opposing sides that give their word yet break them. We have already been given the peace of Jesus, but we let our resistance to it keep us from experiencing it. If we have held on to a grudge against our brother or sister, we are holding on to an obstacle that keeps us from offering our gift at the altar. The clogged artery cannot deliver blood to the heart. The hard heart cannot offer compassion to others in need.

If I hate my brother or sister or pretend to offer a sign of peace when in fact I am holding back, hiding my hatred or disgust, refusing to forgive or to be reconciled with those with whom I am at enmity, then I cannot love the God who opened the floodgates of love and mercy to me.

A familiar story to many families is that of the relationship that deteriorates into stubborn silence. A father refuses to talk to his daughter. A daughter runs away from home refusing to communicate with her parents. A brother alienates a brother. A grandparent is denied access to grandchildren. There are many causes of these situations, some no doubt more serious than others; yet until someone makes the effort to break down the walls in such relationships, there will remain these barriers to peace within families. If we cannot achieve peace within our family, how can we expect to achieve peace on a larger scale. In *Pacem in Terris*, Pope John XXIII reminds us there will never be lasting peace in this world until there is peace within every human heart. Impossible? Not if it comes from the Prince of Peace, not if it rises out of the rightful order of things. We have the responsibility to let peace dwell within our own hearts and to let it grow in our relationships with one another.

In whatever we do, we have such a responsibility. We are called to do whatever we do in the best way we can do it at that moment. If there is an obstacle to our doing what it is we are trying to do, then we are naturally going to be thwarted so long as the obstacle remains.

Of course, we are never going to be able to finish all of our life's work. On the cross, Jesus said, "It is finished." How often can we truly say that our work is finished? How many times have we finished one project only to rush into another? Most of us forget to live today as fully as we might. It is a great loss, if not a tragedy or a colossal comedy, to live it too late. It is equally a loss not to live it at all. "Peacefully do at each moment what at that moment needs to be done." Katharine Drexel is a saint that brings us time and again back to the Gospel. She listened to her master's words, and she listened to the stirring within her own heart. Daily, she lived the Gospel message, and she lived it as one always mindful of her responsibility to contribute to the peacefulness of this world. "Blessed are the peacemakers," Jesus tells us, "for they will be called children of God" (Matthew 5:9).


## REFLECTION QUESTIONS

How do I deal with time? Do I try to fight it by filling it or even overfilling it, or do I not respect enough what I am doing and as a result not meet life fully? What do I need? What can I live without? Do I appreciate the gift of now? What things do I not do peacefully? What keeps me from doing things peacefully or from facing life peacefully? Who have been the peaceful people in my life? Am I aware of the peace of Christ within myself? In others? Do my relationships reveal that I am contributing in a responsible way to the building of a lasting peace in the world? How am I answering the call to greater peace?

# Bibliography

Bristow, Gwen. Interview with Mother Katharine Drexel. New Orleans *Times-Picayune* 15 November 1932, 1+.

Duffy, Sister Consuela Marie, SBS, *Katharine Drexel: A Biography*. Bensalem, PA: Mother Katharine Guild, 1987; originally published in 1966.

Marcello, Leo Luke. *Blackrobe's Love Letters: Poems About Katharine Drexel*. Lake Charles: The Cramers Press, 2000; originally published by Xavier Review Press, 1994.

*Prayers Heard, Miracles Performed: A Special Presentation With Angela Hill*. Video. New Orleans: WWL TV, 2000.

*Praying With Mother Katharine Drexel: Taken From Her Writings*, research by Sister M. Thomasita Daley, SBS, preface by Sister M. Georgiana Rockwell, SBS. Bensalem, PA: Mother Katharine Drexel Guild, 1986.

*Reflections on Life in the Vine, Found in the Writings of Mother M. Katharine Drexel, Foundress of the Sisters of the Blessed Sacrament*. Bensalem, PA: Mother Katharine Drexel Guild, 1983.

Unpublished letters and journals in the Archives of the Motherhouse of the Sisters of the Blessed Sacrament, Bensalem, PA.